# From Martyrs to Murderers

*Jacqueline Dorgan Meketa*

*Other books by Jacqueline Dorgan Meketa*

*Louis Felsenthal, Citizen-Soldier of Territorial, New Mexico*

*Legacy of Honor — The Life of Rafael Chacon,
A Nineteenth-Century New Mexican*

**with Charles Meketa**

*One Blanket and Ten Days Rations*

# From
# Martyrs to Murderers

## The Old Southwest's Saints, Sinners, and Scalawags

by

Jacqueline Dorgan Meketa

*Yucca Tree Press*

**From Martyrs to Murderers: The Old Southwest's Saints, Sinners and Scalawags.** Copyright 1993 by Jacqueline Dorgan Meketa. All rights reserved. No part of this book may be reproduced in any form or by any electronic or mechanical means, including information storage and retrieval systems, without permission, in writing, from the publisher, except by a reviewer who may quote brief passages in a review. Yucca Tree Press, 2130 Hixon Drive, Las Cruces, NM 88005.

First soft cover printing      1993

Library of Congress Cataloging in Publication Data.

Meketa, Jacqueline Dorgan

    FROM MARTYRS TO MURDERERS: The Old Southwest's Saints, Sinners and Scalawags

        1. Southwest United States - History.  2. New Mexico - History.  I. Jacqueline Dorgan Meketa.  II. Title.

Library of Congress Catalog Card Number: 93-060808

ISBN: 1-881325-08-3

Cover design by John Cole of Cole Graphics

# Contents.....

| | |
|---|---|
| Photographs | v |
| Documents and Maps | vii |
| Agony In the Wilderness | 1 |
| The Deadly Chalice | 13 |
| To Feed His Soul With Vengeance | 24 |
| Raton's Black Comedy | 41 |
| A Ghostly Tale | 52 |
| My Mother Is a Murderess! | 64 |
| Mystery Death In the Palace | 76 |
| The *Bandido* and the *Señorita* | 87 |
| A Bloody Afternoon in Santa Cruz | 99 |
| A Singular Friendship | 113 |
| Let Me Die With Honor | 121 |
| A Plethora of Purple Prose | 135 |
| Hillsboro's Scandalous Sadie | 147 |
| With Unflinching Devotion to Duty | 161 |
| The Midnight Stranglers | 174 |
| A Bitter Price | 184 |
| Swept Away By the Deluge | 196 |
| Selected Bibliography | 203 |
| Index | 209 |

# Photographs....

|  | Page |
|---|---|
| Santa Fe in the 1870s | |
| Major James H. Carleton | 10 |
| Governor David Meriwether | 10 |
| A simple adobe church | 14 |
| Archbishop Jean Baptiste Lamy and Rev. Joseph Priest Machebeuf | 16 |
| Rev. Peter J. Munnecom | 20 |
| A traditional Navajo hogan | 32 |
| Cliff dwellings in Cañon de Chelly | 32 |
| Albert H. Pfeiffer in beaded deerskin cloak | 38 |
| Raton street scene | 46 |
| Engine 1222 of the Atchison, Topeka, & Santa Fe | 46 |
| Gus Mentzer's body on public display | 48 |
| Flag pole in Taos plaza | 54 |
| Smith Simpson | 60 |
| Smith Simpson's home in 1920s | 60 |
| Smith Simpson at Kit Carson's grave | 62 |
| Kit Carson's gravestone | 62 |
| Silver City courthouse | 65 |
| Socorro saloon interior | 68 |
| Early day Socorro street scene | 68 |
| Southwest corner of Santa Fe plaza in 1855 | 79 |
| Georgetown-Silver City stagecoach | 89 |
| Georgetown, New Mexico | 95 |
| Basement jail under the Silver City courthouse | 96 |
| Zuñi Pueblo | 103 |
| Cañon de Chelly | 103 |
| General Sterling Price | 107 |
| The Spiegelberg Brothers | 116 |
| Spiegelberg Brothers store | 116 |
| St. Francis Cathedral, Santa Fe, New Mexico | 118 |
| Archbishop Lamy | 118 |
| 'La Conquistadora' | 118 |
| A Mexican salt cart | 126 |
| Luis Cardis | 128 |
| Charles Howard | 128 |

| | |
|---|---|
| Outdoor newspaper office | 136 |
| Early-day Socorro, New Mexico newspaper office | 136 |
| Charles P. Clever | 142 |
| Sadie Orchard's 'Mountain Pride' stagecoach | 151 |
| Kingston, New Mexico street scene | 151 |
| Sadie Orchard on horseback in riding habit | 155 |
| Sadie Orchard in her later years | 155 |
| Sketch of a Buffalo Soldier by Frederic Remington | 162 |
| Colonel Edward Hatch | 166 |
| Troop H, Ninth Cavalry, Ft. Wingate, New Mexico | 167 |
| Navajo scouts at Ft. Wingate | 167 |
| Victorio, Warm Springs Chief | 170 |
| Colonel Ethan W. Eaton | 177 |
| Frenchy Elmoreau and Bush Clark hanging from a cottonwood in Socorro, New Mexico | 181 |
| Socorro, New Mexico street scene | 182 |
| Catholic procession in Socorro, New Mexico | 182 |
| An Apache *rancheria* | 189 |
| Merejildo Grijalva | 192 |
| Apaches visit Washington, D.C., 1876 | 192 |
| Sarah J. (Sally) Rooke | 198 |
| Telephone office in Folsom, New Mexico after the flood | 198 |
| Memorial plaque on Sarah Rooke's grave | 201 |
| Dedication of memorial on Sarah Rooke's grave, May 15, 1926 | 201 |

# Documents & Maps....

| | |
|---|---|
| A contemporary newspaper account of Father Munnecom's case | 18 |
| Military report describing Pfeiffer's condition | 29 |
| Floor plan of the Palace of the Governors | 77 |
| A proclamation of a reward for James Collins' murderer | 82 |
| A letter from Albert Gay to his parents | 101 |
| Map of Albert Gay's travels from September 1, 1847 to March 16, 1848 | 106 |
| Map of the Salt War area | 122 |
| Pay voucher for Sergeant C.E. Mortimer | 132 |

*This book is dedicated to ten special people,*

*my grandsons*

*Deneb, Rigel, Jason, Jeffrey, Antares,*

*Steven, John Tyler, and Jarek,*

*and*

*my granddaughters*

*Madison and Riley*

# Introduction

The virtues and foibles of the human race are fascinating fodder for any writer at any time, but particularly so, it seems to me, when they are recorded from real life. As Byron said, "...for truth is always strange; stranger than fiction."

Over the years, as an historian-writer, I have encountered hundreds of colorful stories in the course of my research, when, with my husband's help, we have scrutinized old diaries, letters, manuscripts, microfilmed nineteenth-century records and newspapers, literally thousands of books, and a variety of dusty documents. While I don't think one can find anything basically different in the character of the present-day populace—it certainly ranges from the depths of degradation to the heights of humanitarian self-sacrifice—I do think that the more austere and primitive conditions of life in the Southwest in the last century add extra color and flavor to the tales of the saints, sinners, and scalawags of those days.

These were God's unpampered people, living in a time and place lacking today's comforts, support systems, and scientific advances. But, although these harsh conditions were sometimes instrumental in determining specific hardships or circumstances, it is only necessary to look beyond the trappings of the story to find the eternal human emotions—heroism, greed, determination, fear, anger, patriotism, revenge, self-indulgence, madness, and all the rest.

While the old records, particularly Territorial newspapers, are filled with curiosity-arousing items, it is a sad fact that, in many cases, the incidents were so briefly reported and the participants so socially insignificant in their time, that no researchable trail was left by which an event could be expanded and examined in more detail. Perhaps this is why the stories of a few of the brave hearts and the black hearts of the past are told and retold.

But I refuse to re-plow the same ground. In this collection you'll find no Billy the Kid, no Sheriff Elfego Baca, no Tunstalls and their Lincoln County War, no Geronimo, and no Sheriff

Pat Garrett. Nevertheless, I believe I have found a group of fascinating but lesser-known people who were all caught up in exciting or unusual events.

Each of the tales has some connection to the New Mexico Territory although, in several cases, most of the action took place outside its borders in other Southwestern states. The protagonists are as varied as the narratives, and their deeds range from the foulest to the finest.

Some of these stories were published previously in western history magazines such as *Old West*, *True West*, and the now-defunct *Real West*, as well as the *New Mexico Historical Review*, an academic journal. It is with gratitude that I acknowledge the editors' permissions to reprint those pieces.

Special thanks must also go to the many, many folks I have contacted during my years of research and writing—staff members of museums, large and small; fellow historians and researchers; archival personnel, both photo and documentary; and librarians. They seemed almost universally as excited and interested in the successful completion of my project as I was, and their courtesy, patience, and generosity of spirit was much appreciated.

But most of my gratitude is directed toward my husband, Charles, who was always willing to take that trip to search out an illusive document, to tramp weedy cemeteries searching for a particular weathered headstone, to snap one more photo under atrocious lighting conditions, or reach down that heavy, dusty tome from an out-of-reach shelf.

A last thought or two: being, as they used to say, "of the female persuasion," I felt it only appropriate to begin and end this book with the stories of two ladies who proved that the "weaker sex" really wasn't.

Come, then, and meet 'Limpin' John, Sally Rooke, 'Bush' Clark and his pal 'Frenchy,' Padre Etienne Avel and the rest. Each has a story to tell.

Jacqueline Dorgan Meketa
Placitas, New Mexico
November 1993

# Agony In the Wilderness

It was a crisp autumn day in 1853. The small party of New Mexican traders, mounted on mules, slowly traversed the vast Southwestern plains, a territory virtually uninhabited except for roaming bands of Indians. They were more than a month into a trading expedition and had seen no other humans for weeks. Suddenly, from behind some brush, there appeared a sight which made them doubt their eyes. Standing before them in this God-forsaken wilderness was a white woman!

True, her hair was chopped so short that her blistered and burned scalp could be seen and her bare feet were bloody and swollen almost double in size.[1] Also, her skin, mostly visible through the few rags covering her body, was darkened by dirt, ashes, exposure to the sun, and the dried blood smeared on it. But, still, without a doubt, she was a white woman, and a young one at that.

The men quickly approached this emaciated apparition and, by using sign language and their native Spanish, a few words of which the woman understood, soon learned that she had escaped from the Comanches twelve days earlier. Since then she had existed on the few hackberries she could find and water from a nearby spring. She was wasted away almost to a skeleton and the coyotes, sensing her weakness, had been edging closer to her daily, anticipating her final collapse.

The sympathetic traders fed her and gave her a blanket and some of their own clothing to wear. Although the pitiful captive undoubtedly felt great relief at being in safe hands, her hardships and suffering were not yet over. It would be almost two more months before the young widow, just turned seventeen, would sit before New Mexico Governor David Meriwether and other officials in the safety of Santa Fe and tell them the story of her ordeal.

Even though some accounts have listed Jane Adeline Wilson's maiden name as Howard, the truth is that she was born in Alton, Illinois, in 1832, one of ten children of William and Jane Smith.[2] Later the family moved to Missouri and then on to Paris, Texas, where the parents suddenly died within one day of each other, leaving their six surviving children, all very young, orphaned. The oldest brother secured homes with various neighbors for the different siblings, including one sister who was a dwarf, a condition the local people attributed to medicine a doctor had once given her. Sadly enough, shortly after his mission was completed, the brother himself died suddenly of "winter fever."

At the age of fifteen, Jane married James Wilson, a nineteen-year-old farmer who lived nearby. The young newlyweds, naive and gullible, heard that people "became rich very fast in California," and decided to travel there with James Wilson's father and three young brothers.[3] They joined a wagon train traveling from Hunt County, northeast of present-day Dallas. All went well until they arrived at the Guadalupe Mountains, approximately one hundred miles east of El Paso, where the Mescalero Apaches stole their nineteen head of cattle.

When the emigrant train arrived at El Paso, James Wilson, apparently angered that the proprietor had not done more to help him regain his stolen livestock, decided to drop out and remain there until the next California-bound party arrived.[4] This proved to be a fatal decision.

# Agony In the Wilderness

El Paso, in those days, was a quasi-settlement which had sprung up on the Texas side of the river opposite the large Mexican town of *El Paso del Norte* (present-day Juarez, Mexico). It was a motley collection of adobe huts, and had come into being as a stopping place for bull freight teams and as a rest stop on the Southern Overland Stage Line.[5] The town had no government, local law, or constable, and was a wild collection of cattlemen, outlaws, footloose explorers, gamblers, soldiers, ladies of the night, and every other sort of transitory citizen.

While the Wilsons waited, light-fingered locals managed to steal most of their other property. Now, practically penniless, they could not go on to California but were forced to make arrangements to return to east Texas. Within days of departing on the return trip to their former home, Jane Wilson's husband and his father were murdered by Indians when they fell behind their wagon train after stopping to repair a broken harness. Young Jane, who was pregnant, then returned to nearby El Paso, where she stayed a month before trying once again to make her way home, taking her three young brothers-in-law with her.

A malignant fate, however, seemed to pursue the grieving widow. She and the boys began traveling eastward with a very small party. After a number of days on the trail, just about the time they were getting close to the safety afforded by the fort at Phantom Hill, Texas, disaster struck. Men from the traveling party stole three animals from the proprietor and ran off. He, anxious to retrieve his property, took the oldest Wilson boy, fourteen, with him and started in pursuit, leaving Jane Wilson, the two younger boys, and a Mexican employee to hurry on as quickly as they could.

About noon the following day, four Comanche braves swooped down upon the defenseless party. Jane and the two boys were quickly taken prisoners. The Mexican's fate was much worse. Jane described events this way:

> After the mules were unharnessed, the Mexican was stripped of his clothing, his hands tied behind his

> back, and ordered to sit down upon the ground. One of them [the Comanches] then went behind him and shot him with a gun, while another stabbed him several times with a large butcher knife. His scalp was cut off before he was dead, and put into his own hat; the hat was then worn by one of his murderers. I was stupefied with horror as I gazed on this spectacle, and supposed that my turn would come next. But the Indians...ordered us to go with them. As I left I looked back and saw the poor Mexican weltering in his blood, and still breathing.

Jane Wilson probably never knew it, but the Mexican teamster, although scalped and shot in the shoulder, survived. Military records indicate he was found by a friendly Comanche who sent word to the fort at Phantom Hill. A relief party was dispatched to bring the Mexican to the post for care and two consecutive patrols were ordered out to search for Jane and her young brothers-in-law, but their efforts proved unsuccessful.[6]

In the days that followed her capture, young Jane Wilson would endure extreme hardship. She had a fine head of hair which she valued very highly. Almost immediately the chief ordered it cut off and, in her own words, "I was not a little mortified in seeing it decorating the heads of the heartless savages. My head was thus left entirely unprotected from the intensely hot rays of the sun."

But much worse yet lay in store. The first twelve days of her captivity, as the party traveled over the plains, Jane described her suffering as "so severe as to take from me all desire to live." Then three other Comanches appeared and joined the group— two braves and an Indian woman. But, instead of receiving compassion from one of her own sex, Jane found that her mistreatment escalated at the instigation of the squaw.

In the beginning, the captive was mounted on an unbroken mule without a bridle. The animal frequently bucked her off over its head. This the chief found inordinately amusing. He, therefore, would shake the Mexican's dried scalp in the beast's face to frighten it and make it rear and throw Jane violently to the ground. This was done as often as six times a day, always to the Indian's great glee. No matter how stunned or badly hurt Jane might be after a fall, her captors would beat her with lariats, sticks, and whips if she did not rise and immediately remount. The Indian woman would also stab Jane with the point of a spear she carried. The fact that Mrs. Wilson was well along in her pregnancy seemed to make the situation all the more comical to the Comanches.

As the Indian's slave the white woman was compelled to carry large loads of wood on her back "which, being destitute of sufficient clothing was mangled till the blood ran down to my feet," she reported. Jane was also required to round up her captor's animals each morning, chasing them on foot and then restraining them until they were wanted. When she could not work well enough or fast enough Jane reported that she was whipped "till my flesh was raw. Large stones were thrown at me. I was knocked down and stamped upon by the ferocious chief who seemed anxious to crush me like a worm beneath his feet. My head sometimes fell under the horses' feet and then the Indians would try to make the beasts kick me."

Forced to go without food for several days at a time and refused permission to drink except when in camp at night, the suffering woman said she "ardently desired death that my torments might come to an end." Her hatred of the chief who inflicted such barbaric treatment, including "every indignity offered to my person which the imagination can conceive," made her feel that "...if I could only cut him to pieces I could die content."

For weeks the Comanches and their prisoners traveled on. Within a few days of their capture Jane Wilson's two young brothers-in-law were given good animals to ride and were supplied with bows and arrows. Their faces were painted in Indian fashion and they were never subjected to any cruelty. In short order they not only looked like young Comanches but seemed to enjoy their new life.

Each night the traveling party camped on a hill or other high ground and Jane Wilson was forced to sleep on the bare earth exposed to the rain and cold autumn winds without benefit of any kind of shelter or covering.

When the mule Jane Wilson was riding eventually became tame enough to cease throwing her the Indians forced her to dismount and begin walking. She said, "The road over which we passed was often very rough and stony, and full of thorns. My feet were wounded and bruised till they were covered with blood and greatly swollen. But still I was obliged to keep up with the rest of the party and if I fell behind I was beaten until I was almost senseless. The Indians often urged me on by trying to ride their horses over me—many a mile of that road is marked with my blood and many a hill there has echoed to my useless cries."

Early each morning the Comanches would force Mrs. Wilson to pack a heavy load on her back and begin walking ahead of them in the direction they pointed out. They would remain resting in camp until later and then overtake her since they were mounted. On the morning of the twenty-fifth day of her captivity, Jane Wilson, worn and weak, decided she would not give her captors the pleasure of watching her die. She hurried ahead as quickly as her condition would allow and eventually found what seemed a suitable place to hide in bushes some distance off the trail. Once they discovered her missing the Comanches searched for a time but finally gave up when they did not find her hiding place.

After the Indians left the area Jane Wilson was overwhelmed by the realization of her situation. In recent weeks she had lost her husband and his family, along with what little property she had in the world. She was now alone on the wild prairie in Indian country, hundreds of miles from civilization, with nothing but the rags on her back. It is also probable that she had already, or soon would, deliver a premature, dead baby as a result of her hardships.

Jane makes no mention of such an event in recounting her ordeal. Such matters, along with the possibility that she was raped while held captive, were delicate subjects that were not spoken or written about publicly in those days. One author did

Santa Fe, New Mexico's "adobe capital," as it looked when the rescued Jane Wilson spent the winter there. (Harper's Weekly, 1879)

declare that she saw Jane Wilson with a baby shortly after her rescue, but this and other assertions she made about the capture and rescue are highly suspect. Also, other accounts of Jane Wilson's stay over the winter in Santa Fe before her return to Texas the following spring make no mention of the birth or existence of a child.[7]

During the next twelve days of frightening solitude Jane Wilson's indomitable spirit kept her alive against all odds until the New Mexican trading party happened upon her—an event all concerned must have felt was miraculous.

The traders, however, faced a dilemma. They could not abort their trip at this point and turn back, but neither could they leave Jane alone in the wilderness. Yet they knew that the Comanches, with whom they hoped to barter, would take the woman back into captivity if they saw her. The New Mexicans mounted her on one of their burros and continued on their way, probably planning to hide her somewhere before they arrived at the Comanche camp.

Two or three days later, however, the trading party suddenly spotted an unexpected band of roving Comanches and were forced to conceal Jane hurriedly in a nearby ravine, promising they would return for her that night.

But when darkness fell the New Mexicans failed to appear. As hour after slow hour dragged by, Jane Wilson became more and more terrified that she had been abandoned once again to die alone on the prairie. Finally, about midnight, the mounting fear and insecurity forced her out to wander about in the pitch darkness searching for the trader's camp. While creeping through some brush she heard the sound of someone approaching. She threw herself to the ground as a Comanche brave passed less than twenty feet away, but he failed to see her. After this terrible fright she lay still for a long time but finally started moving stealthily forward once again. She was eventually discovered by the trading party's herdsman, a Pueblo Indian, who was out checking on the animals.

He told her that their camp was still full of Comanches and that if she was seen the traders would be unable to save her. He made her lie on the ground and covered her with dry grass. She lay there all the next day, unable to move, and the following night crept forth to quench her almost intolerable thirst. The herdsman returned, under cover of darkness, and brought her some bread, warning her that under no condition was she to leave her hiding place the next day.

All the following day, as time seemed to stand still for the immobile hidden woman, she could hear Comanche braves passing to and fro, calling to one another as they remained in camp. Finally, that night, the herder was able to sneak out to her once again. He brought a blanket and several loaves of bread and told her the trading party was being forced by the Indians to travel further on, probably to the Comanches' major camp, and they would be gone for at least seven or eight days.

The next morning, as she watched her new-found friends disappear, Jane Wilson was flooded once again with hopelessness. Only a few days earlier her life had seemed spared by Divine Providence after she had resigned herself to death. Now, once again, all chance of rescue seemed to be disappearing over the horizon.

But Jane Wilson, despite the almost unbelievable string of catastrophes which had befallen her in her first sixteen years, still had a reservoir of strength and determination to tap. She soon rallied, and resolved to survive as long as possible. She discovered a large log which had been left burning in a nearby ravine and tended it night and day to keep the fire going, because without it she would have frozen to death in the bitter November weather.

Nearby, the stranded girl found a hollow cottonwood stump which she covered with bark and leaves to keep out the freezing wind. She told of that time, saying, "This stump was my house during my stay here. When I could endure the cold no longer I would leave my house and run to the fire, but was afraid to stay there long lest the Indians should see me. The wolves soon found out my place of retreat and frequently, while I was in the stump, they would come and scratch around and on its top. The hackberries were very scarce here, and had it not been for the bread Juan Jose gave me I do not see how I could have kept from starving to death."

After eight days of isolation, cold, hunger, and alternating hope and anxiety, Jane Wilson heard human voices calling to one another. Unsure whether or not they were Indians, she crept out cautiously and joyfully found the traders who had been unable to remember exactly where they had left her. They were shouting at each other hoping to attract her attention.

Once reunited with the kind and caring New Mexicans, Jane Wilson's tribulations were over. The men mounted the emaciated woman on their finest horse for the thirty-four-day trip back to civilization and treated her with civility and solicitude. When they reached the town of Pecos, New Mexico, they turned the rescued woman over to the care of several military officers, including a Lieutenant Adams, whose wife donated clothing from her own wardrobe for Jane's use, and Major James Carleton who, in a few years, would become the Commanding General of the Department of New Mexico.[8]

Word of the rescued woman was then sent to Governor David Meriwether in Santa Fe. He immediately dispatched his

## Martyrs and Murderers

James H. Carleton was a young Army major in New Mexico in 1853 when he aided the recently rescued Jane Wilson. (Museum of New Mexico)

David Meriwether when he was Governor of New Mexico Territory from 1853-57. (Museum of New Mexico)

son, Raymond, with a mule and borrowed side saddle, to escort her to the capital city. After her arrival, Governor Meriwether personally arranged that she be outfitted with a complete wardrobe of new clothing and boarded in the home of a respectable Methodist lady. The following Spring the governor also paid for her passage on a wagon train back to her friends in Texas. The entire amount he expended in helping Mrs. Wilson was $360, for which the government eventually reimbursed him.

According to reports, Jane Wilson's young brothers-in-law, aged ten and twelve at the time of their capture, were ransomed later from the Comanches and delivered to authorities in Texas.

In the years that followed, Mrs. Wilson dropped into relative obscurity. Over time, however, her adventures were written about by various authors who often embellished and embroidered them to a considerable degree. It is doubtful that she would have been pleased if she had known of this notoriety. She was described at the time of her trials as "intelligent, although youthful in manner, modest and retiring, a truthful person who did not volunteer a relation of her sufferings but rather shrunk from making them public; the account was only drawn from her by repeated questions."[9]

It is a sad fact that, by the tender age of seventeen, Jane Adeline Wilson had suffered more pain, loss, sorrow, humiliation, and hardship than most of us do in a lifetime. Her indomitable spirit marks her as a heroine deserving respect and honor.

Endnotes:

[1] Most of the details describing this incident were selected from the December 24, 1853, issue of the *Santa Fe Weekly Gazette*, which contains Jane Wilson's personal account of her capture and captivity. The complete newspaper article was reproduced, with minor editing, in a booklet published in 1971 by Ye Galleon Press of Fairfield, Washington, under the title, *A Thrilling Narrative of the Sufferings of Mrs. Jane Adeline Wilson During Her Captivity Among the Comanche Indians*.

## Martyrs and Murderers

The 1853 issue of the *Weekly Gazette* contained an impassioned editorial about Mrs. Wilson's ordeal and the need for the Indians to be punished. The article was written by James L. Collins who was, with that issue, severing his connection with the newspaper and its editorial conduct. It is ironic that Mr. Collins' own unfortunate future would ensure that his death would become another of the stories which comprise this book.

[2] In *My Life In the Mountains and On the Plains* (Reprint; Norman: University of Oklahoma Press, 1965) p. 219, former New Mexico Governor David Meriwether made this error and a number of others. Mistakes from his account, which was written from memory some years after the events, were picked up and reiterated in other books such as Hobart E. Stocking's, *The Road to Santa Fe* (New York: Hastings House, 1971) p. 154.

[3] *Santa Fe Weekly Gazette*, December 24, 1853. All future quotations, unless otherwise noted, will be from this source.

[4] A proprietor was the person with a vested interest in the majority of the animals and contents of a wagon train, and who originally established it. Because there was security in numbers, it was not unusual for unaffiliated or smaller groups to arrange with these owners to travel with established trains. A wagon master, on the other hand, was merely an employee in charge of one or more wagons.

[5] Robert J. Casey, *The Texas Border* (New York: The Bobbs-Merrill Co., 1950) pp. 29-32.

[6] Jerry Thompson, *Henry Hopkins Sibley: Confederate General of the West* (Natchitoches, Louisiana: Northwestern State University Press, 1987) pp. 99-100.

[7] See *Land of Enchantment, Memoirs of Marian Russell Along the Santa Fe Trail as Dictated to Mrs. Hall Russell* (reprint; Albuquerque: University of New Mexico Press, 1981) pp. 33-36. Russell mentions seeing a red-haired woman with a baby at the stage station in Albuquerque and identifies her as Jane Wilson. However, many of the details she recounts about Mrs. Wilson are incorrect, i.e., that she had twin sons who were killed by the Indians, etc. In addition, Governor Meriwether's account enumerates in detail arrangements he made for Jane Wilson's care in Santa Fe and return passage to Texas, and presumably would mention an event as notable as the birth of a child if it had occurred.

[8] By 1862, shortly after the close of Civil War activities in the territory, Carleton became the military commander who instigated and oversaw the roundup and dispatch to reservations of the Navajos and Apaches of the area.

[9] This judgment of Jane Wilson's character was part of the December 24, 1853, *Weekly Gazette* article and presumably was the opinion of Editor Collins.

# The Deadly Chalice

It was August 3, 1858, when the energetic priest, his black cassock flapping against his legs, hurried across the sun-baked yard and into the rather primitive adobe church in the small town of Mora in northern New Mexico. For some reason, Father Pieter Jan Munnecom, who was regularly scheduled to celebrate the nine o'clock services for the assembled faithful, was temporarily absent. So Father Avel, not wishing to have the parishioners wait, was filling in at the last moment.

Entering the dimly lit interior, illuminated only by daylight filtering through several small windows high on the walls, the padre, Etienne M. Avel, first went to hear the confessions of a few waiting parishioners. He spoke their native Spanish with ease even though he was a Frenchman. He, like Father Munnecom, had arrived in New Mexico four years earlier to work as a missionary with Bishop Jean Baptiste Lamy, who was radically changing the role and activities of the Catholic Church in this formerly Mexican-held territory.

On the hour, when Munnecom, the Dutch priest, still had not returned, Father Avel began the Mass himself. All proceeded normally until Father Avel took the chalice with the

A simple adobe church, probably much like the one in Mora where Father Avel died. (Author's Collection)

consecrated wine and raised it to his lips to partake of it as part of the communion ceremony. He drank only a small quantity and realized immediately that it had a "singular taste" and was somehow polluted.[1] He remarked upon the unusual flavor and sent the acolyte to the sacristy for fresh wine but, within moments, became aware that he had been poisoned.

The faithful flock of dark-eyed señoras with shawl-covered heads and simple peon-farmers watched, first with surprise and then with mounting fear, as the determined priest tried to complete the Mass even though tremors began to shake his body. Then, in anguish, he cried out to them,

"Pray for me. I am dying poisoned!"[2]

A man named Noel, present in the church at the time, rushed up to the altar and assisted the stricken clergyman into the sacristy where he attempted to give him an antidote. It was said that, at the same time, he informed Father Avel that the younger priest, the Reverend Munnecom, must have poisoned the wine in revenge for the appointment of Avel to his parish to replace him. Munnecom had been only a seminarian when he arrived in New Mexico but, after ordination in Santa Fe, was assigned as Mora's first pastor when it was established as a parish two years earlier.

There was great confusion and excitement among the shocked parishioners gathered around the fallen pastor. Someone in the crowd suggested that Father Munnecom be found and brought to the church to give the dying priest the last sacraments but Avel refused, saying, "I cannot confess to a priest who has poisoned me."[3]

Less than fifteen minutes after drinking the wine the popular priest was dead. Before succumbing he had been able to make an informal will leaving the books he owned to Bishop Lamy and his fiscal assets, three thousand dollars, to establish Santa Fe's first hospital which would open eight years later. His last act, before dying, was to forgive his murderer.[4]

The following Saturday, the *Santa Fe Weekly Gazette* ran a brief article describing the incident in which it stated, "Padre Avel was a popular priest universally liked by members of his Church and our citizens generally. He was considered one of the most talented and highly educated priests in the Territory and his melancholy death is generally regretted."[5]

The little town of Mora, almost exclusively Hispanic and Catholic, was horrified and astounded at this turn of events. True, murders certainly were not unknown. There probably was not a man, woman, or even child in the village who had not seen first-hand the results of a brutal, bloody killing of some sort. In addition to the run-of-the-mill violence most frontier towns experienced, Mora residents had been dealt other blows in recent years.

Eleven years earlier, in 1847, local insurgents still rankled by the American occupation of New Mexico two years earlier, killed some Americans in the village. A short time later, eighty United States soldiers were sent into town seeking the culprits, and a battle took place, in which a captain and two of his men

Archbishop Jean Baptiste Lamy (standing, center left) with Right Rev. Joseph Priest Machebeuf (standing, center right). Both men were originally convinced of Father Munnecom's guilt.
(Farrar Collection, New Mexico State Records Center & Archives)

were slain. In retaliation, the military attacked the hamlet and burned it to the ground.

Also, only two years before the priest's death, Apaches surrounded Mora, kidnapped some women and children to be sold into slavery, and took practically all the horses, sheep, and goats in the high mountain valley. Indeed, life was hazardous and tenuous in that place and at that time but *for a holy man to be killed, in the sanctity of the church, on the very altar, and at the moment of communion*, was so mind boggling it was no wonder that wild rumors flew through the community like autumn leaves in a windstorm.

The prime suspect, of course, was the unhappy Father Munnecom, thanks to the unflagging efforts of the parishioner Noel who was casting suspicion on him with the speed and determination of a stoker fueling a roaring furnace. Within a

## The Deadly Chalice

day or two of the murder, Noel abandoned the care of his sheep and pastures and left hastily for the town of Las Vegas to the south. There he managed to intercept Vicar General Joseph Machebeuf, who was hurrying to Mora to investigate the case since Bishop Lamy was away on a trip.

Noel told Machebeuf that Father Munnecom had been jealous of Avel and implied it was very strange that the Dutch priest had not been present to say the Mass as scheduled. Apparently, he skillfully projected the image of a bereaved and concerned parishioner who had been a great friend of the deceased priest, and who felt no rancor against Munnecom but only sadness. At any rate, he managed to cast enough aspersions that Machebeuf, and later the bishop in turn, were convinced of Munnecom's guilt. Bishop Lamy wrote, "We suspect, with good reason, not a Mexican priest, but an unfortunate Dutch priest...."[6]

But, strangely enough, the vocal Noel never returned home to his land and animals in Mora; he disappeared completely. Then suspicion began to fall upon him. It was said that when Noel's common-law wife fell ill and was dying he sent for Father Munnecom to administer the last rites. Munnecom had been replaced as pastor by Avel, but was still in Mora assisting in the work until he received a new assignment. And, at that particular moment, Avel was away on a mission visit so the Dutch priest was the only one available to be summoned to the sick bed.

Munnecom, acting as a strict cleric with a European background, was not sympathetic to the more lax ways the Mexican priests had allowed for many years in the isolated and primitive outpost of New Mexico. He refused to visit the woman unless she renounced her lover. As death approached, the desperate woman finally consented. She sent Noel away, was given absolution, and died. It was said that Noel, distracted by rage and grief, threatened revenge against the Dutch priest. People now began to see events in a new light, and wondered if Father Munnecom had been the intended victim and if pure chance had placed Padre Avel on the altar after the chalice had already been poisoned.

# From Martyrs to Murderers

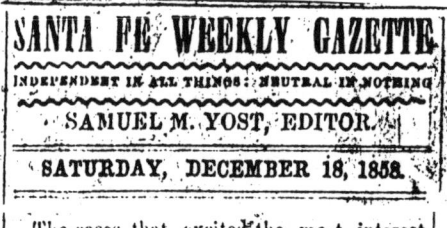

A contemporary newspaper account of Father Munnicom's case.

Was this why Noel had been present at the Mass and rushed forward so anxiously to aid the stricken priest, desperately attempting to reverse the poison's action with an antidote? Was this why he had gone to such lengths to convince the dying priest and the bishop's representative that Father Munnecom was guilty? And was this why he left his home and worldly goods?

Perhaps. But other villagers were equally convinced that Father Avel's death was the work of a closed religious society organized earlier in New Mexico. This was during the period when the area was the northern province of Mexico and lacked sufficient clergy to minister to the needs of the people. Without

# The Deadly Chalice

formal religious leaders, some of the citizens established an organization known as *Los Hermanos de los Penitentes*, or Brothers of Penance, who fasted at Easter time, beat each other with cactus whips in penance, and reenacted the crucifixion with great realism. Forbidden to continue their practices, first by Mexican Bishop Zubiria and later by Bishop Lamy and his priests when they arrived to take over the reins of Catholicism in the territory, the brotherhood went underground. Some of the locals believed that certain of the society's members had felt it necessary to eliminate the bothersome priest who, they suspected, was determined to crush their secret sect.

To this day there is still a legend in the Mora area to bolster this theory. According to the story, when the priest was about to consume the lethal altar wine, a woman in the congregation, who knew of the plot but was unable to allow the *Penitentes* to take this sort of revenge, suddenly cried out a warning. It is said that the priest had such a strong faith that he replied calmly, without even turning his head, "'Tis the consecrated wine of the sacrifice of the Mass," and drank the potion expecting that its blessed condition would save him from any harm.[7]

Father Avel's murderer was never caught. Because of the unsophisticated conditions of the place and time no efficient investigation was promptly carried out and, as a result, any useful evidence was lost. In addition, the waters became so muddied by rumor, unprovable accusations, gossip, and wild theories that little reliable information was available.

Noel was never seen in Mora again, but many years later news came that he had been murdered in southern New Mexico. After living under a devastating cloud of suspicion for two years, the Reverend Munnecom was cleared of murder charges following an investigation by the chancery and the courts. He served as a pastor elsewhere in New Mexico for several years and was then assigned to the rapidly growing mission church in Trinidad, Colorado.

But once again the story takes a strange twist. Instead of being a pious, dedicated cleric living by the same uncompromising rules he imposed upon the dying woman in Mora, Father

# From Martyrs to Murderers

Rev. Peter J. Munnecom was always a controversial priest, first in Mora, New Mexico, and later in Trinidad, Colorado. (Author's Collection)

Munnecom turned out to be a high-liver who flagrantly ignored the conventional dictates for priestly behavior. He arrived in Trinidad in June, 1866, to find a crude church built of adobe blocks with a dirt roof and bare earthen floor. Most of the congregation were devout Mexican-Americans who had come to settle Trinidad from Mora County, New Mexico. As a result, they were painfully aware of the story of the murder of Father Avel.[8]

This, however, was the least of Father Munnecom's problems. Even though the handsome, curly-haired priest began calling himself Pedro Juan, the Spanish version of his Dutch name, he continued, with rigid persistence, to act in the same ways which had alienated him from the Hispanics in Mora. He still did not become fluent in Spanish, and he refused to modify his attitudes to better understand the temperament and customs of the local people.

In addition, and probably worst of all, he established a scandalously profligate life style. For example, on Christmas

# The Deadly Chalice

Day in 1867, after completing the Mass, he, the town doctor, and several other cronies first attended the cock fights in order to wager on their favorite birds and then retired to one of the local watering holes for some serious drinking and poker playing.

Father Munnecom was reported to be a regular at the periodic all-night card games where the participants "played for blood and stayed at it until just after dawn, when a devout Mexican layman tolled the church bell to summon the faithful and the celebrant to Mass. The padre, to the delight of his fellow players and anyone else within hearing, always said the same thing when he threw his cards down: 'There goes that damned bell again.'"[9]

Munnecom's actions infuriated the local Catholics and antagonized Bishop Machebeuf as well, and if it had not been for an extreme shortage of priests it is highly unlikely that he would have stayed in Trinidad as long as he did. Finally, in 1875, after "years of tippling, playing poker, transacting business deals, and fattening his pocketbook, Padre Munnecom was replaced by two dedicated Jesuits."[10]

For several years after his ouster, the Hollander stayed in Trinidad as a businessman, remaining close to his old socializing pals. He eventually returned to his native Weert in Limburg, but even after he left Trinidad many of the Protestants and Freemasons, who had long maligned him, continued their gossip. Many hinted that the Church was aware that Munnecom really had murdered Father Avel and, in a conspiracy, had been keeping him in the sparsely settled area of southern Colorado. Another totally fictitious tale which was repeated for years said that, upon his departure, Munnecom had taken one of the local nuns with him and that they were living in sin in St. Louis.

In Mora itself, time and other important events tended to push the memory of the case of the murdered priest into the background. In the 1860s it was the Civil War and Indian fighting which required many of the local men to leave home and serve in the military. A decade later violence and terrorism spilled over into Mora from the nearby town of Las Vegas, which harbored cut-throats and rascals with such exotic names as Scar-face Charlie, Rattlesnake Sam, Jack-knife Jack, Cock-eyed Frank, and the Pock-marked Kid.

Although Father Avel's murder remains one of the most bizarre mysteries in New Mexico history, the story is not widely known. Equally puzzling as who murdered him is the question of where Father Avel was buried. The Santa Gertrudis parish church, where he died, has been replaced by two successive church buildings, the latest of which was dedicated in 1972, but no evidence of him exists there. The Archdiocese records in Santa Fe provide no clues as to the location of his grave.

Hispanic residents of northern New Mexico, however, have incorporated the story into their folklore. Through old poems, songs, and tales, mostly told in lyric Spanish, they have retained much of their culture and history, and the legend of Padre Avel is repeated to each new generation along with other narratives about the old days and the old ways.

## Endnotes:

[1] *Santa Fe Weekly Gazette*, August 7, 1858.

[2] Paul Horgan, *Lamy of Santa Fe*. (New York: Farrar, Straus and Giroux, 1975), p. 260.

[3] Ibid.; and Ray John de Aragon, "Mora Intrigue and Murder," *New Mexico Magazine* 60 (August 1982), pp. 32-34.

[4] Horgan, p. 260; Sytha Motto, "Women's Role In Shaping State Goes Way Back," *Albuquerque Journal* Bicentennial edition, February 1, 1976; and Reverend W. J. Howlett, *Life of the Right Reverend Joseph P. Machebeuf, D.D.* (Pueblo, Colorado: The Franklin Press Co., 1908), p. 241.

[5] The citizens of Santa Fe knew Father Avel very well. When he arrived in the city with Lamy from France in November 1854, he remained there working on the cathedral staff and ministering to the people for four years. He also served briefly at Albuquerque and Socorro before being reassigned to Mora shortly before his death. Avel, who had been ordained in Clermont, France, in 1844, obviously was older than Munnecom who was only a seminarian when he arrived with the same party of European clerics.

[6] Horgan, pp. 260-61.

# The Deadly Chalice

[7] Stanley F. Crocchioli, *The Mora, New Mexico, Story* (Pep, Texas: n.p., 1963), pp. 8-9.

[8] Rev. Anthony J. Adams, S.J., *Holy Trinity Church Centennial: 1885-1985* (Trinidad, CO: n.p., 1985), p. 1.

[9] Barron B. Beshoar, *Hippocrates In A Red Vest* (Palo Alto, CA: American West Publishing Co., 1973), p. 101.

[10] Ibid., p. 164.

## To Feed His Soul With Vengeance

The huge Navajo warrior, young and powerful, strutted back and forth, daring the Tabeguache Utes to find him a worthy opponent. As he moved, muscles outlined under his smooth copper skin hinted at great strength. This was why he had been chosen by his tribe to represent them in a battle to the death.

Several days earlier the two large bands of Indians had arrived simultaneously at the site of a nearby thermal spring, highly prized for its healing waters. Since then they had been involved in fierce combat over the right to use their constant 153-degree waters. Finally, with matters at a stalemate, they agreed to settle the question of ownership once and for all with a Bowie-knife duel between individuals representing each tribe.

Partisans ringed the clearing where the deadly combat would take place. Now the Ute leaders pushed through to present their fighter. A murmur of surprise and disbelief arose. He was a small, wiry, white man who would never see forty again—an adopted tribal member.

Both men stripped naked, armed themselves with the knives and, ringed by the tribesmen, began their awful battle. As they circled, feinted, and maneuvered for a deadly strike, the blades flashed in the high-mountain sun. Albert Pfeiffer, the white man, small and lithe, darted here and there with the dexterity of a determined terrier as the larger, slower Navajo lunged violently at him.

Suddenly Pfeiffer found an opening, sprang forward, and sank his heavy blade deeply into the chest of his opponent, striking the heart, and in moments the young warrior lay dead. In one of the unique events in Western history, a white man had earned for the Utes the exclusive right to the waters of Pagosa Springs, Colorado. Some years later, when, by treaty, the Utes ceded portions of the area for white settlement, Pfeiffer made an unsuccessful claim to ownership of the spring, declaring he had been instrumental in obtaining it for the tribe.

Today, a bronze plaque embedded in a stone monument marks the site, but Albert H. Pfeiffer's appreciation of his immortalization would probably be somewhat hampered by the fact that the inscription reads, "Col. *Alfred* H. Pfeiffer."

But, dramatic and life-threatening as the incident might seem, it pales beside another incredible occurrence, five years earlier, which once again involved Indians, a therapeutic hot spring, and Albert H. Pfeiffer.

It was June, 1863, when the small party of soldiers and civilians stopped at a small thermal spring near the Rio Grande in southern New Mexico. Captain Albert H. Pfeiffer, in command of a company of New Mexico volunteers from nearby Fort McRae, ordered his escort of six soldiers to post themselves on nearby rock outcroppings as lookouts. He knew the vicinity was a favorite fording spot for Apaches moving stolen livestock to their mountain strongholds.

Pfeiffer's wife, two servant girls and a civilian friend spread out rugs and raised blankets to protect themselves from the scorching desert sun. Pfeiffer undressed and immersed himself in the hot mineral waters, hoping to gain relief from the inflammation and pain of the severe facial skin affliction which had driven him here.

Some time later the placid scene was violently torn apart. A party of Apaches, almost twenty strong, after circumventing the guards, sprang to their feet, simultaneously whooping and firing as they attacked. Two of the soldiers were killed immediately and another wounded. The others fled in panic. Pfeiffer, naked and his side pierced by an Apache arrow, leaped from the water, grabbed his rifle, and fired, killing one of the attackers.

The pitiful screams of the women, now being seized by the Apaches, tore at Pfeiffer's heart but, as the only man armed and standing, he knew he would be dead within moments if he tried to fight against the overwhelming odds. Almost twenty years' experience with Southwestern Indians made him gamble that the Apaches might not immediately kill the captured women but would take them prisoners. He decided to attempt an escape by running to the Rio Grande, crossing, and struggling the seven miles back to Fort McRae to give the alarm.

But the Apaches had no intention of making it that easy for him. They gave pursuit, firing their weapons at him again and again as the bare-footed Pfeiffer raced away over sharp stones, through cactus, and over the rugged, uneven terrain, the arrow still protruding from his body. Soon realizing he had no chance of outrunning or eluding his enemies, the desperate Pfeiffer halted and made a stand. At this point he spotted a natural enclosure of rocks. For several hours, the Indians tried unsuccessfully to close in on him without losing any of their warriors to his sharpshooting. Meanwhile, the fair-skinned forty-year-old captain, a Dutchman from the northern coast of Holland, was scorched by a desert sun blazing in the cloudless sky. Finally, fearing the eventual arrival of troops from the fort, the Apaches left.

Wounded and sun-seared, Pfeiffer quit his rustic fortress, determined to make his way back to Fort McRae. Propelled by his rage at both the Indians and the soldiers he felt had abandoned him and by the tormenting thoughts of his wife's peril, the officer pushed forward over the cruel desert, sometimes running, sometimes trotting, and sometimes staggering, but always blindly advancing. But even before his arrival, other survivors had reported the ambush to the fort's commanding officer, Major Arthur Morrison. Morrison personally headed up a party of twenty mounted men and rushed out in pursuit.[1]

Albert Pfeiffer was more dead than alive by the time he reached the post. The Army surgeon was appalled when he saw the man's condition. Although he managed to extract the arrow successfully, he could do virtually nothing but watch helplessly as great patches of Pfeiffer's burned and blistered skin peeled away from the man's body, a result of the terrible sunburn he had experienced.

To add to his torment, the suffering man was soon notified that his wife's body had been found along the trail where she and the others had been attacked and left to die by the Apaches, who wished to disencumber themselves as the pursuing soldiers closed in. The final bitter pill was that the Apaches had then separated and melted into the vegetation and arroyos, escaping unscathed.

Then, almost unbelievably, a malevolent destiny, dissatisfied with prostrating Pfeiffer both physically and emotionally, bestowed even more painful news. Word was received at Fort McRae that, on the very day he and his wife had been assaulted, Pfeiffer's second-in-command and close friend, Lieutenant L. A. Bargie, was killed by other Apaches some miles to the south. Bargie, with a detachment of seven of the company's enlisted men, was headed toward the post with a wagon when the attack came. Bargie and another man were slain and two other soldiers wounded. The details were even more bitter for Pfeiffer to hear. An officer reported that when the corpse of Lieutenant Bargie was found, "...his head [was] cut off, his breast cut open and his heart taken out—it was an awful sight—I shuddered, such a sight I never beheld before."[2]

Adding to Pfeiffer's grief and anger was the fact that he had not wanted to go to the hot springs at all but only did so as the result of a report written by an Army inspector who had recently examined the small outpost and its personnel. It said, in part:

# From Martyrs to Murderers

> Captain Pfeiffer is an old soldier who served well & faithfully, and is a very honest, honourable & upright man, anxious to do his duty. He is afflicted with a painful & annoying disease upon the face, which I have no doubt in a great measure prevents his giving proper attention to his company...I advised him to have medical treatment...to go to the Hot Springs which are reputed to be efficacious in diseases of the skin. He declined, upon the plea that he was anxious to go with his Regiment upon the Navajo campaign... and seemed to think the present was no time for him to leave his company...I am, nevertheless, of opinion that he should be allowed an opportunity to restore his health; and respectfully recommend it.[3]

The inspector was being very circumspect. He knew his report would be seen by Christopher 'Kit' Carson who was the commanding general of the New Mexico Volunteers. He also knew that Pfeiffer and Carson were as close as brothers and even though Pfeiffer had been doing a lot of heavy drinking he dared say nothing more than, "An inspector, unacquainted with him, might very naturally come to the conclusion, from his personal condition & state of his company, that he was both morally & physically incapacitated."

Carson, however, was aware of Pfeiffer's problems and, on that very day, wrote a letter in which he told Pfeiffer he had just deeded over a parcel of his land to Pfeiffer's son, his godson, as a gift. He went on to say: "I have been making inquiries of every person who has seen you and they all tell me that your face is not yet well, and that you are again drinking. When will you have sense? Can't you try and quit whisky for a little while, at least until you get your face cured? If your face ain't well when I next see you, you had better look out.... Remember me kindly to Mrs. Pfeiffer, and remember also what I say about your drinking."[4] So it is probable that Pfeiffer, out of love and respect for Carson, and knowing that the inspection report would soon reach him, had gone to the hot springs in search of a cure.

> English well, seemed to be a capable man, and ... ...
> informed that he had served an enlistment in the Regular Army.
>
> Of Capt Pfeiffer, as regards his personal qualifications, I feel it my duty, though reluctantly, to speak. He is an old soldier who served well & faithfully, and is a very honest, honourable & upright man, anxious to do his duty. He is afflicted with a painful & annoying disease upon the face, which I have no doubt in a great measure prevents his giving proper attention to his Company. I advised him to have medical treatment, and told him that, if he wished it, I would endeavour to procure him permission to go to the Hot Springs, which are reputed to be efficacious in diseases of the skin. He declined, upon the plea that he was anxious to go with his Regiment upon the Navajoe campaign, or to meet the Texans should they again invade the country; and seemed to think that the present was no time for him to leave his Company. I am, nevertheless, of opinion that he should be allowed an opportunity to restore his health; and respectfully recommend it. His case presents some features of hardship. He has served, almost continuously, since July 1861, having resigned, for the purpose, the Abiquiu Indian Agency, and has received pay only since last November. For fourteen months service he has received nothing whatever. Maj. Morrison stated privately that

A portion of the military report, dated May 8, 1863, which describes Capt. Pfeiffer's physical condition just prior to his visit to the hot springs. (National Archives)

## From Martyrs to Murderers

After the tragedy of his wife's death, Albert Pfeiffer was a changed man. It was later written that this "mild-mannered and kindly" fellow was transformed into "a very paladin of the frontier...probably the most desperately courageous and successful Indian fighter in the West."[5] No one can know the mental anguish, grief, burning hatred and frustration in his mind while the captain lay immobilized and ineffective during the five weeks of recovery. Years later he wrote, "Some [of my men] run away and after my recovery I could not find them in my Company because I would have Killed them for their Cowardice to leave me alone."[6] Whether they deserted or were transferred away to save their lives is not known.

As soon as he had healed sufficiently to travel, Pfeiffer was back in command of his Company H and looking for revenge. Undoubtedly much of what was said or written about his proclivity for dispatching red men was exaggerated, but his first action, as soon as his body was well enough to allow him to sit in the saddle, was to join Carson at Fort Wingate in western New Mexico in early August to participate in the military endeavor to subdue the Navajos and place them on the Bosque Redondo Reservation. It was reported that Carson sympathetically humored him and that it mattered not to Pfeiffer whether he hunted down Navajos or Apaches; a hostile was a hostile.

Only two days after joining Carson, Pfeiffer was out with scouting parties, searching for Navajos and carrying out the scorched-earth policy of destroying Indian crops. Within days he had captured twelve Navajo women and two children and seized one thousand head of sheep and goats. Pfeiffer personally severely wounded an Indian brave who "contrived to secrete himself in the rocks" and could not be found. Several days later, however, Moqui Indians reported the death of the wounded Navajo, saying he was not only one of the most powerful but also the worst chief of the Navajo nation.[7]

Throughout the summer the military concentrated on pursuing the Navajos in unrelenting fashion. As winter came upon the land, the now-hungry and harassed Navajos suffered more and more. Wishing to take advantage of their desperate plight,

## Feed His Soul

General Carleton ordered Carson's New Mexico Volunteers to step up their campaign even though they, too, were suffering greatly.

"I will venture to assert that no troops of the United States have ever before been called upon to endure as many hardships as did the men of my command," Carson would write.[8] But General Carleton, safe and warm in Santa Fe, wanted success. When the Indians ran off part of the mule herd and the horses became unfit, the order still was to go, "*Now*, while the snow is deep." It mattered not that the men, on scouts for weeks, had to endure long marches, some at night, carrying all their supplies on their backs. They struggled through snow eighteen inches deep and still falling, with temperatures which dropped well below zero. They were issued only one shoddy blanket and bivouac fires were forbidden, lest the Indians know of their presence.

On January 6, 1864, while the entire area was covered with a deep snow, Colonel Carson again left his new headquarters at Fort Canby with a large command. He ordered Captain Pfeiffer out independently, with approximately one hundred men, to reconnoiter the east opening of the *Cañón de Chelly,* the magnificent red sandstone canyon in northeastern Arizona which had long served as a home and fortress for the Navajos. The spectacular canyon had never been breached by white troops who, in the past when chasing Navajos, glanced timorously at its sheer walls and then retreated in haste, seeing it as a death trap.

Carson, himself, planned to march to the canyon's other opening and thus bottle up the Indians. Before leaving headquarters Carson sent out an ox train of supplies headed for his eventual camp at the west end of the canyon. The snow drifts were so deep that twenty-seven of the animals perished from exhaustion before they had gone twenty-five miles. Held up by the weather, Carson's command was not able to reach *Cañón de Chelly* until January 12. Once there he could find no sign of Pfeiffer's detachment.

Uneasy, the next morning Carson sent out two columns of troops, one along each rim of the great crevasse, to reconnoiter

(*above*) A traditional Navajo hogan, round in shape, windowless, and with the entrance facing to the East. (*below*) The almost perpendicular walls of Cañon de Chelly in northeastern Arizona made it a Navajo fortress never traversed by white men until Albert Pfeiffer's daring exploit. (Author's Collection)

the terrain all the way to the eastern end. They were to search for Indians, and try to find Pfeiffer. No trace of Pfeiffer's party was found. Puzzled and now deeply concerned, Carson returned his troops to camp. There they found the missing contingent and learned they had penetrated the entire length of the canyon without a single casualty! In fact, the day he exited the canyon, Pfeiffer captured nineteen Navajos who approached him under a flag of truce. The exploit was so awe-inspiring Carson's men seized Captain Pfeiffer, put him on their shoulders and carried him around camp amid the wildest rejoicing, with cheers and shouted congratulations filling the air.

Many, although filled with admiration, felt that Pfeiffer was courageous to the point of being foolhardy. They knew what a bold move this had been, for the Navajo easily could have hemmed the soldiers in or laid a successful ambush in the depths of the canyon. Indeed, several days later one hundred fifty adult Navajos surrendered at that spot.

In a detailed military report Captain Pfeiffer described his experiences in the canyon. He wrote that, as they traversed the extremely narrow portion of the canyon, they encountered "Indians on both sides, whooping, yelling and cursing, firing shots and throwing rocks down upon my command" and stated that they had killed two male Navajos and one woman in that encounter when they "obstinately persisted in hurling rocks and pieces of wood at the soldiers." He also described how the agile Indians were able to "jump about on the ledges of the rocks like mountain cats, hallooing at me, swearing and cursing and threatening vengeance on my command in every variety of Spanish they were capable of mastering."[9]

Once their last stronghold and sacred place had been breached, the already desperate Navajos began to surrender in large numbers. They told Carson that their people were in a complete state of starvation, and that many of their women and children had already died from this cause. Many of the troops, seeing the ragged and gaunt women and children prisoners, felt great pity.

## From Martyrs to Murderers

The achievement of being the first to traverse the *Cañón de Chelly* and the subsequent victory over the Navajos was reported to Washington. Captain Asa Carey, who went through the canyon several days after Pfeiffer, was recommended for a brevet promotion. One contemporary author stated, "Captain Pfeiffer the audacious was officially overlooked; but he did not care. Others could have the honors; he would write his own record with bullet and knife and feed his soul upon the spoils of the vengeance trail."[10] This exemplifies the reputation which was becoming attached to Pfeiffer. Actually, Pfeiffer was later brevetted a major of volunteers for "gallantry in marching and fighting his way against Navajo Indians through the whole length of the *Cañón de Chelly*."

Pfeiffer's penchant for recklessness and daring during the six-year-period of his service as a New Mexico volunteer officer was the stuff of which legends are made. One lieutenant who served under him for a brief period described Pfeiffer as a fighter who never got into a scrape with the Indians without being wounded and another account stated that Pfeiffer's body bore no fewer than seventeen scars attributable to bullet and arrow wounds.

Once the Navajos were subdued and forced on the long march to the Bosque Redondo Reservation, General Carleton turned his attention toward the still-troublesome Arizona Apaches, saying he planned to wage "a general war" against them "to insure a lasting peace, and a security of life to all those who go to that country to search for the precious metals."

Carleton utilized mostly New Mexico and California Volunteer soldiers for the task. Pfeiffer and his company, as part of the Apache Expedition, were attacked by a band of Indians near the *Colorado Chiqúito* (Little Colorado River), in northern Arizona, in June, 1864. In a running fight of eight miles, the soldiers managed to kill five and wound seven Apaches. After the battle, the cavalrymen made camp. Some time later two Indians approached their bivouac, displaying signs of peace.

As they drew close the Apaches suddenly lowered and fired their guns, severely wounding Captain Pfeiffer in the leg and grievously wounding a private. Pfeiffer's men, whom he had at the ready, returned fire and the Indians were killed instantly. At the sound of the shots, a large, hidden party of Indians came running toward the camp. On Pfeiffer's shouted command, a volley was fired into them, wounding several, and the rest scattered in all directions. For this action, Pfeiffer was later brevetted a lieutenant colonel.

After recuperating, the indomitable Pfeiffer returned to duty. In the summer of 1865, he served as Carson's second-in-command at the newly-established Camp Nichols on the Cimarron cut-off of the Santa Fe Trail. Camp Nichols was created to help safeguard traveling caravans from raids carried out by the Kiowas, Cheyennes, and Comanches. Pfeiffer had almost complete charge of the outpost since Carson was already suffering periods of pain from the aneurysm which would, within a few years, cause his death. When Carson was called to Washington to testify at the Sand Creek Massacre hearings, Pfeiffer was left in complete charge. After the summer travel season the camp was abandoned.

The following winter, when word was received at military headquarters in Santa Fe that three Indian children had been murdered by some Utes, it was Pfeiffer who was called upon by General Carleton to investigate the matter. Major Pfeiffer, unable to receive any supplies or assistance from the Indian Agent in charge, nevertheless set out on the mission on his own through snow two-feet-deep. Pfeiffer would later write about being "...such a great fool to go out...this whole concern cost me about $300 more out of my Pocket besides being nearly frosen [sic] almost dead and run a great change [sic] for my top Knot..."[11]

But Pfeiffer was not always heroic. One incident was reported from Fort Garland, Colorado, where, by autumn, 1866, he, Carson, and a regiment of volunteers were stationed because of Ute unrest. Since Pfeiffer and others had a tendency to abuse "spirits," Carson issued an order to the post sutler saying no liquor was to be sold to anyone except by his express order.

## From Martyrs to Murderers

One beautiful sunny day Carson decided to enjoy a carriage ride with his wife and children and was absent from the post for a few hours. Pfeiffer, the next highest ranking officer, decided that, in Carson's absence, he was in command. He issued a counter-order and sent for ten gallons of liquor for his own use.

Three or four hours later, when Carson returned, he found the whole place on "a grand old frolic—nearly everybody drunk." The irate Carson immediately called upon the sutler and was presented with Major Pfeiffer's counter-order.[12]

Summoned for an explanation, Pfeiffer pled ignorance "with the technicalities of military rule," saying he thought he had as much right to issue the counter-order as Carson had to initiate the original one. As usual, with magnanimity, Carson let Pfeiffer off with a severe reprimand after receiving his promise that the incident would not be repeated.

By late 1867, however, both Pfeiffer, by then a brevet lieutenant colonel, and Carson, a brevet brigadier general, were discharged from the military. On the eve of being mustered out Carson wrote Pfeiffer a letter, calling him a "dear...intimate and esteemed friend" and recalling that he had "...long learned to place in you my confidence as an officer and a man." Carson said Pfeiffer's "knowledge of frontier and Indian life in this country is unsurpassed" and his courage "too well known to need any endorsement of mine." The following spring, when the now seriously ill Carson moved his family to a settlement on the Purgatory River in Colorado, it was his close friend, Albert Pfeiffer, who accompanied and assisted him on the trip.

What was the origin of this man who became known as "the scourge and terror of the Indians in time of war and their *Tata* Pfeiffer in time of peace?" Pfeiffer was born in Friesland, on the northern coast of Holland, in October, 1822. His father was a Lutheran minister and his mother reportedly descended from a Scottish noble family.

Pfeiffer left his native land at the age of twenty-two and, after arriving in America, journeyed westward to St. Louis. Soon he made the trip over the Santa Fe Trail to New Mexico, probably as an employee of one of the freighting outfits supplying the Mexican-American War effort. At the close of the war,

Pfeiffer became a trader, opened a business in Santa Fe, and joined the local Masonic organization. In 1855, Pfeiffer joined the New Mexico Battalion of volunteers as a lieutenant. He participated in the six-month-long Ute War in southern Colorado, fighting bands of Utes and Jicarilla Apache. The fighting was carried on during the winter in bitter cold and deep snows, through high mountain passes and narrow defiles, and the soldiers suffered great hardships. The Indians were finally defeated and forced to the treaty table. Kit Carson was chief guide for the military command and this may have been the point at which his life-long friendship with Pfeiffer began.

By 1859, Pfeiffer was the Indian Agent at the outpost of Abiquiu in north-central New Mexico. It was there that he met his *señorita*, the only love of his life, whom he would marry. Antonita's father operated a trading post in the settlement and her wedding dress was one of the most expensive seen in the Territory up to that time. It was made of yards and yards of heavy white satin, all hand-embroidered at the convent. Red roses literally covered the cloth, and the white tulle veil was caught here and there with white flowers. She wore a necklace of gold filigree set with precious stones from which hung a gold fish pendant with jeweled eyes and valuable pearl scales.[13]

The couple had several children before her terrible death at the hands of the Apaches near the hot springs in 1863, but only one, a son, survived to adulthood. Albert Pfeiffer never married again.

In July, 1861, Pfeiffer resigned his commission with the Abiquiu Indian Agency to join the New Mexico volunteer regiment then being raised to counteract the invasion of the Confederate Army of Texans, which hoped to conquer the Territory. In early 1862, he fought bravely, with Carson, against withering Confederate fire at the bloody Battle of Valverde. Afterward he, Carson, and many others, remained in the military to fight the Indians. It was during this period that he lost his wife to the Apaches.

After that tragedy and his subsequent determination to fight Indians, a mystique about him began to grow, fueled by storytellers with fertile imaginations. One tale related how, on one

## From Martyrs to Murderers

Albert H. Pfeiffer wearing the beaded deerskin cloak he reportedly took from a Comanche chief he killed in a mounted, running battle. (Museum of New Mexico)

occasion in Santa Fe, he "wrapped a *serape* around his head, ran into a store that was on fire, and brought out two kegs of powder which were charred and blazing." Another yarn, wickedly exaggerated, had Pfeiffer, after the death of his wife, making frequent month-long trips alone, except for his horse, trusty rifle, and half a dozen wolves, into Apache country from which he would return "seemingly pleased. 'They like me,' he once said of the wolves, 'because they're fond of dead Indian and I feed them well.'" Such embroidered accounts were not unusual, told either around campfires or printed in Territorial newspapers.

One report regarding Pfeiffer's pursuit of Indians, however, seems to have concrete evidence to back it up. He was said to have come upon a band of Comanches from Texas out on the plains and opened fire upon them. The mounted Indians swung their bodies down on the far side of their horses as they galloped, shielding themselves by horse flesh from Pfeiffer's bullets. Pfeiffer singled out the chief and managed to maneuver to a position where he was able to shoot him in the back. The chief was reported to be wearing a beautifully beaded deerskin cloak which the captain took. Pfeiffer proudly sat for a photograph wearing a cloak which was covered by Indian folk-lore symbols—stars, moon, gourds, snakes, and trees—all worked in beautifully colored beads sewn on with deer sinew. Two small bullet holes in the back of the garment reputedly bore evidence of Pfeiffer's marksmanship.

In actuality, Pfeiffer, like Carson and most of their peers, had no hatred for the Native Americans except for the tribal warriors, who were their natural enemies in combat. Often they were more generous, kind, and compassionate toward the Indians than the civilians who neither understood nor had faced them in battle.

At the conclusion of his military service, Albert Pfeiffer returned to an area he had first encountered in 1851 and fallen in love with, describing it as "the finest country I ever saw." Here, in a valley near Del Norte, Colorado, he developed a ranch on his land. He was a respected and popular citizen who, on occasions, enjoyed a good game of chess. He was associated with a number of cattlemen whose large herds were sometimes allowed to winter on Ute meadows because of the tribe's high esteem for Pfeiffer. Still, the hardy scout was unable to settle completely into the consistencies of ranch life, and was often absent from home for long periods, "off with the Indians."

One day, in the summer of 1879, while working with some horses at his ranch, Pfeiffer was kicked and his leg broken just below the knee. Although he was reported doing well after medical attention, this incident marked the beginning of declining health for the old pioneer.

By autumn of the following year, the fifty-nine-year-old Pfeiffer was bedfast, and in the months that followed it became increasingly clear that the former soldier, who had bounced back from so many assaults upon his body, was not going to recover this time. On April 6, 1881, Albert Pfeiffer died. His last request was that he be buried quietly and simply. Only five people were present when he was interred, without ceremony, in the pinon-studded foothills overlooking his beautiful ranch.

Endnotes:

[1] Laura C. Manson White, "Albert H. Pfeiffer," *Colorado Magazine* 10, No. 6 (1935); 217-22.

[2] Extract of a letter by Lt. Wm. Hofedank to Capt. Ben C. Cutler, Las Cruces, N.M., June 20, 1863, "Letters Received by 9th Military District, Dept. of New Mexico and District of New Mexico, 1849-1890," Microfilm Collection, Special Collections, University of New Mexico, Albuquerque.

[3] Ibid., Capt. A. W. Evans to Asst. Adj. Gen. Headquarters, Department of New Mexico, Franklin, Texas, May 8, 1863.

[4] Col. C. Carson to Pfeiffer, Santa Fe, N.M., May 8, 1863, Edwin L. Sabin, *Kit Carson Days, 1809-1868* (New York: Press of the Pioneers, 1935), pp. 617-618.

[5] A.A. Hayes, Jr., *New Colorado and the Santa Fe Trail* (New York: Harper Bros., 1880), p. 166.

[6] Albert H. Pfeiffer to John Gwyn, Costilla, N.M., September 13, 1870, New Mexico State Archives and Record Center, Santa Fe, N.M.

[7] Sabin, pp. 866-67. In what context the Moquis were describing the dead Navajo as the "worst chief" is not clarified in the military reports.

[8] Carson to Cutler, December 6, 1863, *War of the Rebellion*, Series I, Part 1, Vol. 26, p. 255.

[9] Capt. Albert Pfeiffer to Lt. Lawrence G. Murphy, Acting Asst. Adj. Gen., Navajo Expedition, *War of the Rebellion*, Series I, No. 34, Part 1, pp. 76-78.

[10] Sabin, p. 723.

[11] Pfeiffer to John Gwyn, October 7, 1870, La Costilla, Colorado Territory, Albert H. Pfeiffer Papers, New Mexico State Records Center and Archives, Santa Fe.

[12] Ritch Papers, Huntington Library, San Marino, California.

[13] White, p. 217.

## Raton's Black Comedy

As events unfolded one Monday night in Raton, New Mexico, more than a hundred years ago, it looked like a hilarious performance from a screenplay for a Keystone Cops comedy. But, unfortunately, the bullets were real and the fallen men did not get up and walk away when the action was over.

There are perhaps half a dozen accounts of what transpired that night in the high mountain town near the Colorado border, and no two seem to agree on all major points.[1] Some, without a doubt, were embellished in the retelling, but all relate a macabre series of events which result in quite a story.

According to the local newspaper, the evening's tranquility was broken and the series of events set in motion about 7:00 p.m., when Gus Mentzer, "under the influence," as usual, stopped Deputy Sheriff R. P. 'Pete' Dollman in front of the Bank Exchange Saloon. Mentzer pulled his gun, thrust it under the deputy's left arm and against his ribs, and demanded that the lawman give up his own gun. The deputy refused.

The reason for Mentzer's action is unknown, but his rash deed was probably a result of inebriation, along with pent-up anger at having been discharged from his position as barkeeper/part owner at the Bank Exchange Saloon a short time before.

Six months earlier a gentleman named William Burbridge had come to Raton and rented a newly-constructed building with plans to fit it out as a "model bar and billiard hall."[2] He ordered three sideboards from Cincinnati at a cost of nearly a thousand dollars, decorated the place with marble, cut glass, and French mirrors, and named it the Bank Exchange Saloon. Some accounts say that originally Gus Mentzer was Burbridge's partner in the establishment and that the two men were from Texas where Mentzer had fought a duel to save Burbridge's life. Whether this is true or whether Mentzer was merely an employee, Gus's enchantment with the bottle and propensity for carousing caused the older, more settled Burbridge to dissolve their business arrangement and throw the twenty-four-year-old out on his ear.

Immediately after that event the chagrined Mentzer had left town, but now he was back and apparently simmering with resentment. At any rate, he had Deputy Dollman in a precarious position when a nearby citizen named Johnson leaped forward and struck Mentzer's arm, making his pistol discharge at the ground. The startled Mentzer then turned and ran toward the door of the Bank Exchange Saloon. Dollman quickly fired several shots at the fleeing man, missing him entirely, but managing to wound a Mr. H. W. Harris in the leg. This innocent passerby had been hurrying down the street to the doctor's office to summon medical attention for his son who was very ill at home. Meanwhile, according to the account in the Raton newspaper, Gus Mentzer ran through the saloon, out the back door, made his escape, and a long search failed to turn up the miscreant.[3]

Other versions of the beginning of Raton's night of insanity, however, are much more hilarious. One scenario had all the action occurring inside the saloon when Burbridge refused an irate Mentzer's challenge to duel and the intoxicated young hothead reached for his pistols. Deputy Dollman, seeing this, was supposed to have shouted out a warning to Burbridge while beginning to draw his own gun. Burbridge, however, was reported to have misunderstood the deputy's intent, to have pulled his own sidearm and begun to fire at the lawman while the inebriated Gus started to shoot at everyone. Soon a general melee purportedly erupted.[4]

Another version stated only that the two ex-partners emptied their revolvers wildly at each other while terrified saloon occupants dove for cover or fled out the door. Either way, such a fusillade would have been awe inspiring with the din of the rapid firing, the crashing of furniture knocked over by swiftly departing patrons, the sharp jangle of breaking glass, the acrid odor of black powder and the sulfuric gun smoke quickly filling the room.

Regardless of the number of participants, it was reported that when the last bullet was fired and silence descended upon the scene, it was discovered that everyone present was unscathed, except for Mentzer, who had sustained a very minor injury. The bar, however, was purportedly mortally wounded; most of the glasses and liquor bottles smashed, the saloon's water system shattered, and even the skylight overhead hit and splintered by an errant bullet.[5]

Within moments, Gus, his guns temporarily out of ammunition, was said to have whirled and run out the door. As soon as the stunned bar patrons recovered they reacted by quickly giving chase in the form of an informal posse led by the very angry deputy, Dollman.

Gus, who sometimes also was referred to as 'The Kid,' was observed heading for the railroad depot and soon someone reported he had been spotted hiding behind some piles of freight. But, just as the irate crowd arrived, so too did the evening train. The unprepared passengers were probably quite surprised when an armed band of citizens suddenly climbed aboard and begin searching through the cars. All the various accounts do agree that the villain seemingly disappeared into the deepening twilight and could not be found even after an extensive search.

# From Martyrs to Murderers

Hunting down a troublemaker can be exciting, especially when there is only one of them and you are part of a throng, but it can also be thirsty work. Soon the crowd gave up the search and adjourned to the Little Brindle Saloon (since the Bank Exchange Saloon was such a mess) where Deputy Dollman bought the first round for all the members of his spontaneous posse.

For the next hour or so drinks flowed freely, some bragging was done, and there was much speculation about how far Gus Mentzer would travel before he dared show his face in another town. Then, as the story goes, it was decided to return to the Bank Exchange Saloon to examine the damage at the scene of the "Great But Bloodless Shootout."

At that point, the unbelievable happened. Bold as brass and lively as ever, in strode Gus 'The Kid' Mentzer. He calmly pushed his way through the astonished crowd in the ravaged watering hole, approached the bar, and ordered a hefty potion to wet his whistle. Whether he got his libation and had time to toss it down has not been recorded for posterity, but what happened next was reported in some detail in Territorial newspapers.

Once the flabbergasted patrons realized what had actually occurred they rushed at the scoundrel. Mentzer pulled two pistols, ran out the door to the middle of the street, and then turned and faced the sidewalk. As some of the bar patrons followed him out they opened fire. In a ridiculous replay of the earlier incident, Mentzer once again headed for the railway depot, running backward part of the time and returning fire at the furious crowd in hot pursuit.

While all this was going on, a performance of "Only A Farmer's Daughter," starring the Wallace Sisters, was underway at the nearby McAuliff & Ferguson Hall. Most of the town's respectable citizens were in attendance, dressed in their best bibs and tuckers. The thespians, emoting in a most tragic manner, had captured their audience's total attention when suddenly the first shot was heard outside and then, in rapid succession, at least twenty more. Panic erupted in the hall, women were screaming and crying, and in moments, "the house was broken up and people rapidly dispersed in fear and trembling."[6]

Oblivious to the massive yet comic uproar occurring behind him, Mentzer raced to the railroad yard. At this point, however, things were about to turn from ludicrous to lethal.

When Mentzer reached the platform of the section house a local citizen, H. J. Latimer, who was standing there, pulled out his gun and the two men exchanged shots. Latimer was hit twice, through the knee and in the chest, and badly wounded. Shortly thereafter he was seen staggering down the street crying, "For God's sake help me."[7]

Mentzer then ran across the tracks. Standing there was a switch engine, Number 311, steam up and ready to roll. On board was the engineer and his wife who had just finished buying groceries in town. Mentzer ran around the massive engine and suddenly stopped. Seconds later the first town pursuer, S. H. Jackson, turned the corner and shouted, "There he is!" Just as he uttered the words Mentzer felled him with a fatal bullet through the throat.

Mentzer then quickly climbed into the locomotive cab and frantically began pushing and pulling various levers in a vain attempt to get the engine rolling. The frenzied Mentzer failed to notice the engineer had left the locomotive in neutral. There was pandemonium as the shouting crowd began to surround the engine. Almost immediately a second man, Hugh Eddleston, appeared and began to climb up into the locomotive's cab. Without a moment's hesitation, Mentzer stuck his gun in the man's stomach and dispatched him with one shot.[8]

Now the desperado was in real trouble. He was out of ammunition, two of the town's best-known citizens lay dead, and a crowd with vengeance in its heart had him surrounded. Within moments Deputy Sheriff Dollman mounted the cab of the engine and succeeded in overpowering and arresting Mentzer. He was taken—where else?—to one of Raton's many saloons, the Little Brindle, jointly owned by his victim, Jackson, and his captor, Dollman, who happened to be Jackson's brother-in-law as well as business partner.

*(above)* Raton, at the time of Gus Mentzer's wild escapades, was well supplied with saloons along its main street. *(below)* Engine 1222 of the Atchison, Topeka, and Santa Fe line in the Raton railroad yard where several of the shootings took place.
(Museum of New Mexico)

## Raton's Black Comedy

There Mentzer was left in the custody of William A. Burgen, a recent emigrant from Canada who had been made deputy of the nearby coal mining town of Blossburg only a few days earlier. It was only by chance that Burgen was visiting his brother in Raton that evening when Dollman called on him for help. Dollman, who assumed the whole affair was now ended, felt secure in leaving the prisoner and deputy behind locked doors and went to telegraph Jackson's widow to inform her of her sad new status. Burgen then began to apply leg irons to assure that Mentzer would make no more dashes to the railway station that night.

If, to that point, the evening's events had been preposterous, now they were about to become inconceivable. While the deputy was busy fettering his prisoner, one of Raton's most prominent citizens, the local justice of the peace, Harvey Moulton, appeared. He, too, was a saloon owner; in fact, it was his partner, Eddleston, whom Mentzer had shot in the stomach as he tried to climb aboard the train. Moulton was in no mood to await conventional justice — he wanted immediate custody of Mentzer so he could be measured for a rope necktie. Confronted by the locked door, Moulton violently kicked it in, entered, and shouted, "Give up the son of a _____ to be hung!"[9]

Deputy Burgen refused Moulton's demand to turn over the culprit, stating that it was his sworn duty to hold the prisoner for a legal trial. Moulton, enraged, lunged for the prisoner and the deputy pulled his gun and fatally shot him. Moulton reeled, and, as he fell, managed to get off a shot which hit the officer in the stomach.

Gus Mentzer, hardly able to believe his good luck, surveyed the gory scene and the two downed men, quickly slipped off his shoe, slid his foot out of the shackle, and, free once again, took off out the back door like a scared rabbit.

This time Mentzer shunned the railroad yards, possibly in error, for the third time could have been a charm. Instead he headed through town and darted into a nearby butcher shop. There the fugitive was re-captured. Providentially, the butcher had on hand a long and stout rope which he handed over to the crowd along with the prisoner, according to one account.[10]

## From Martyrs to Murderers

As far as the assembled townspeople were concerned, enough was enough. Taking no more chances they fashioned a noose, slipped it over the killer's head and led him, fighting, cussing, and screaming down the main street to the front of the bank.[11] There the end of the rope was thrown over the ten-foot-high bank sign, which was attached on one side to the building and, on the other, to a sturdy post on the outer side of the plank sidewalk.

Without ceremony Gus Mentzer was hoisted heavenward, but not for long. Down came the poorly attached sign along with the culprit and his hemp necklace. Desperation fueled the crowd's determination to be done, once and for all, with Gus. They chose a young boy who had been observing events with wide-eyed awe, boosted him to the top of the sign post, and had him fasten the end of the rope to it. And thus, Gus Mentzer was finally sent to meet his Maker.

Gus Mentzer's body was still on public display the morning after his hanging. (Amon Carter Museum)

The body was left hanging from the post overnight by the irate inhabitants as a symbol to other lawbreakers. It may not have been a totally effective deterrent, however, if the rumors that someone with a larcenous bent climbed the post during the night and stole three hundred dollars out of the dead man's pocket are true.[12]

It seemed only appropriate, considering the funny/sad chain of events which had occurred, that a final absurdity would transpire. Sure enough, it was later reported that a couple of indigent Raton residents were hired, for a dollar, to dig a grave for Gus Mentzer. However, after laboring for a short time, they decided that an excavation large enough for the coffin would require too much effort on their part so they removed the body from its receptacle, dropped it into the small grave, took the box home and made a cupboard out of it.

The little town was left stunned and shaken by the night's events which had sent five men to eternity, left a sixth seriously wounded, and a seventh slightly injured. All the dead had succumbed quickly except for the unfortunate deputy, Burgen, who was reported to have suffered great agony throughout the night until ten o'clock the following morning when he died. Little hope was held out for the life of the wounded J. H. Latimer but finally, almost a month later, the local newspaper reporting his condition was "improving and it is now thought that he will recover."[13]

In the aftermath of the carnage a number of things occurred. The town turned out en masse for the funerals of Eddleston and Moulton. All businesses were closed, the Santa Fe Railway shops were shut down, and after the services a long funeral procession, lead by the Raton Band playing a dirge, wound its way to the cemetery a mile out of town. Eddleston and Moulton were characterized as "old engineers together... partners in business...and murdered with but a few moments intervening. Inseparable in life they died and were buried together."[14]

Pete Dollman resigned his position as deputy sheriff to give his entire attention to running the Little Brindle Saloon. It was also discovered that a gambler named Turner had, for some ulterior motive, supplied the drunken Mentzer that night with the firearms he used in the shootout and encouraged his original rage. Turner was arrested in the nearby town of Springer but was only fined twenty dollars and court costs and allowed to go free.

Whether it ever occurred to the town's citizens that six of the seven principals in the tragedy, the exception being Burgen, were saloon owners is unknown. But Raton's citizens were so shocked by the events of that bloody night that they passed a public resolution saying they wanted to clean up the town. It read, "...in order to take the first proper step in this matter and show that we are determined and mean just what we say, all professional gamblers, footpads, thieves, cappers, dance hall men, bunko men, and all those who have no visible means of support, as well as all dance house girls and prostitutes generally, are hereby notified and publicly warned to leave this town within 48 hours from...the first day of July, 1882."[15] How thorough the cleanup was and how long the resolve remained effective cannot be said, but the same issue of the newspaper reported that all the gambling equipment from the Bank Exchange Saloon had been sold and carted away to the town of Springer and that 'Billy' Burbridge and his wife were departing the next day for San Francisco.

Raton has long been identified as the town at the base of the high and dangerous mountain pass of the same name which was the last difficult spot to be traversed by Santa Fe Trail travelers before they reached the easier and final leg of the journey southward into Santa Fe. But it should also be remembered as the town where a deadly black comedy took place on June 26, 1882.

Endnotes:

[1] Many variations on everything from the spelling of the principals' names to the sequence of events can be found in the variety of sources used

for this piece. Probably the most accurate accounts can be credited to the local weekly newspaper, the *Raton Guard*, which contained contemporary stories. But even that periodical prefaced its version by saying, "To get at the exact facts during such a state of excitement is almost impossible, but as near as they can be ascertained they are as follows:". Even at the time, other Territorial newspapers wrote highly imaginative stories, including one in the *Santa Fe Daily Democrat* of June 28, 1882, in which a reporter supplied the twenty-four-year-old Mentzer with a long fictional criminal career and a married daughter. A 1932 interview with a Raton old-timer was even more colorful and varied, and articles by later historians seem to gild the story even more.

[2] *Raton Guard*, February 10, 1882.

[3] *Raton Guard*, June 30, 1882.

[4] Kenneth Fordyce, "The Law In Their Hands," unpublished manuscript, WPA American Guide, File 5, D 4, Folder 6, Museum of New Mexico Library, Santa Fe.

[5] Stanley F. Crocchioli, *Desperadoes of New Mexico* (Denver: World Press, 1953), p. 216.

[6] *Raton Guard*, June 30, 1882.

[7] Ibid.

[8] In the Fordyce manuscript, informant A. E. Fairbanks stated that a "Mr. Eldison" was killed first with a shot "in the esophagus" and that "Mr. Jackson" was slain when Gus "...stuck his gun in Jackson's stomach and pulled the trigger."

Several historians and writers subsequently wrote accounts depicting events in this sequence. However, testimony given at the coroner's jury and also an article in the town newspaper, published several days after the killings, both reported that events transpired as written here, with Jackson dying first.

[9] Ibid., pp. 5-6.

[10] Ibid. While the Fordyce account is undeniably entertaining, it contains enough provable errors to categorize it as a mix of fact and fiction, apparently based on an old man's fanciful recollection.

[11] The *Raton Guard*, June 30, 1882, stated, "It is said that Mentzer fought like a tiger while he was being roped and hung."

[12] This report came from A. E. Fairbanks who related his memories to Kenneth Fordyce in 1936.

[13] *Raton Comet*, July 21, 1882. Eleven days after Latimer was shot, the *Raton Guard* of July 7, 1882, stated that his condition was not very encouraging and that recovery was doubtful. Three months after the event, Latimer was said to be well once more.

[14] *Raton Guard*, June 30, 1882.

[15] Ibid.

# A Ghostly Tale

Some years ago a ghost suddenly materialized before the startled eyes of a guest staying in the old adobe building which houses the Harwood Foundation in Taos, New Mexico. The frightened visitor saw that the apparition was a man dressed in knickers and a military tunic. The spirit spoke, saying, "I just thought you should know I was here," and then vanished through a solid wall.[1]

Other reported sightings of this apparently benign specter have occurred over the years. Instead of causing screams of terror from the patrons, researchers, or librarians utilizing the facilities of the art museum-library-meeting place, he is viewed as a sort of colorful addition to the historic structure. After all, these modern-day citizens are guests in his former home, for the ghost has been identified as Captain Smith H. Simpson, a celebrity in Taos during his lifetime who has managed to remain one even now, almost three quarters of a century after his death.

Smith Simpson's local fame, however, is not based on these spooky materializations from some nether world, but rather on his actions while he was very much alive. The most well-known incident occurred in 1861, when the Civil War was tearing the country apart and causing heightened emotions which turned friends into enemies. The tiny settlement of Taos, nestled in the pine-covered mountains between Santa Fe and the Colorado border, was far from the bloody battlefields in the East—but even there, passions ran high.

Ever since the United States had conquered the territory in 1846, the American flag had flown daily from a short flagpole on the plaza in the center of town. But once the Civil War began, local Southern sympathizers repeatedly tore it down.

Smith Simpson, a staunch Union man, soon decided he had had enough. Leading a group of accomplices, he made his way to Taos Canyon where they selected a very tall, slender cottonwood, which the men felled, trimmed, and carried back to the plaza. Although somewhat crooked, it was sturdy. With the help of his friends, Kit Carson, Ceran St. Vrain, Thomas Boggs, and other now-famous mountain men, Simpson nailed the flag to the pole. It was then raised aloft to the accompaniment of cheers from cohorts and Northern patriots.

To emphasize his determination in the matter, Simpson spread the word around town that anyone who dared molest the flag would be shot. In addition, to assure that their country's banner remained undisturbed, the group went to St. Vrain's nearby store and from there took turns standing guard.

Since the flag was nailed to the cottonwood, it flew day and night instead of being lowered at dark. When military officials in Santa Fe learned of the incident, they permitted Taos to fly the flag twenty-four hours a day. As a result of the actions of Simpson, Carson, and the others, Taos today boasts the distinction of being the first place in the United States, by tradition, to fly Old Glory day and night.

Smith Simpson was a colorful character and a dedicated patriot who, more than once, put his life in jeopardy for his beloved country. The adventurous and self-reliant Simpson was born in New York City on May 8, 1833. He was the grandson of a Revolutionary War soldier who accompanied George Washington the night he made his famous Delaware River crossing.[2]

# A Ghostly Tale

Even today visitors to Taos will see the American flag flying day and night in the Taos plaza, a tribute to Simpson's patriotism more than 125 years ago. (Elaine Querry photo. Courtesy of The Taos News)

When Simpson was in his early teens both his parents died of cholera. The boy set out to make his own living, working first in Pennsylvania and then later traveling to New Orleans where he obtained a position as a clerk. Several years later young Simpson moved on to St. Joseph, Missouri, where he was hired to work as second clerk in the service of the Chief Quartermaster for New Mexico. This employment resulted in a trip over the Trail to Santa Fe, where he resided for a year.[3]

On Christmas Day of 1854, the occupants of the small trading post at Fort Pueblo, Colorado, were massacred by a band of Indians. This act resulted in a punitive expedition against the Indians, which became known as the Ute Campaign of 1855. When Lieutenant Colonel Ceran St. Vrain recruited a battalion of volunteer soldiers in northern New Mexico, Simpson immediately enlisted as a commissary sergeant.

The enlistees would see service for six months, from January to July 1855. During that time Kit Carson was the chief guide for the command. The soldiers chased and engaged the Muache Utes and Jicarilla Apaches throughout the rugged mountains of south central Colorado during one of the most bitter winters the area had experienced in a long time.

The twenty-two-year-old Simpson was described in his military records as five feet eight inches tall, with fair complexion, blue eyes and auburn hair. At one point in the campaign, the troops encountered the Apaches at Saguache, where they were entrenched, waiting to give combat.[4] A pitched battle then ensued during which Simpson received a gunshot wound in his right leg and lost his pistol when he fell after being hit. The Indians were reported, by another participant, to have "offered great resistance and fought with reckless valor."[5] It was not until many days later, when the command made its way back to Fort Massachusetts, Colorado, that Simpson was able to receive medical attention and have his wound dressed properly. He nevertheless continued to serve on active duty with his unit, until it was disbanded in July when the Indians sued for peace.

After his discharge, Smith Simpson's wanderlust continued. He ran a government express for several years, a job which

## A Ghostly Tale

required him to ride all over the West through much hostile Indian territory. Then, in 1857, he was off to Mexico City, and later to Brownsville, Texas, then on to New Orleans, and finally back to his native city, New York. There he ran into an old friend, an Army captain in the quartermaster corps. Apparently the pull of New Mexico was still strong, and soon he had hired on, once again, as a clerk and returned to Santa Fe.

Although busy and happy in Santa Fe, Simpson could not rid his mind of memories of Taos, the singularly beautiful village he had first seen during his military service of 1855. The town, situated at an altitude of seven thousand feet, was not only blessed with an abundance of natural resources, invigorating climate, and impressive physical beauty, but was also the home of men like St. Vrain and Carson, whom he knew and admired. Simpson decided to make Taos his home.

Life in Taos suited Simpson. He settled on a farm and kept busy with agricultural pursuits and stock raising. In his free time he often helped his friend, Kit Carson, with some of his clerical work or bookkeeping. It was during this period that the still-remembered flag-raising incident took place.

In view of his strongly evident Union sympathies, it is surprising that Smith Simpson did not join the volunteer forces which were raised in New Mexico in 1861 to defend the area against the invasion of a Confederate force of Texans. After all, St. Vrain was the regiment's first commander and, when he resigned, Kit Carson assumed leadership. Additionally, many of the men Simpson had served with in 1855 officered companies in the new force. But Simpson remained on his farm in Taos while New Mexico's version of the Civil War was fought and finished.

In late 1863, however, military headquarters decided to raise a new regiment of infantry volunteers. These soldiers would be used against the Indians, both to keep the Santa Fe Trail safe from the Plains tribes and in an attempt to control the hostile Apaches of Arizona and southwestern New Mexico. It was at this point that Smith Simpson decided to return to the military life.

(*left*) After his return from fighting Apaches in Arizona, Smith Simpson became one of Taos' leading citizens. This oil portrait, now cracked with age, was painted in his middle years.
(Author's Collection)

(*below*) Smith Simpson's house as it looked in 1920. It is here that his ghost is said to still roam. Burt Harwood photo, Harwood Foundation of Univ. of New Mexico)

## A Ghostly Tale

Simpson was able to recruit enough men in the Taos area to fill a company. Most of the personnel were Spanish-speaking Hispanics native to the area. Simpson was commissioned a captain. After his company had completed its training at Fort Union, it received orders to go on active field duty as part of the Apache Expedition which was to be sent to Arizona.

As the first step, the unit was forced to march four hundred miles southward, mainly following the Rio Grande, until it arrived at the town of Las Cruces, only a few miles north of the Mexican border. This was the headquarters and staging area for the movement of men and supplies westward. The weary soldiers were allowed only a four-day respite before they shouldered their packs again and headed for Arizona. There they stopped at a point on the Gila River, not far from the present-day small town of Geronimo where they established Fort Goodwin, which began as nothing more than rough brush huts the men constructed to protect themselves from the elements.

For the next two years, while on duty in the Arizona Territory, Captain Simpson and his men were involved in numerous long scouts against the Apaches. It was difficult and hazardous duty trying to chase and capture the ingenious Indians in their home territory, filled with inhospitable deserts and rugged mountains. Compounding the problems for the soldiers were the constant shortages of rations for the men and feed for the animals, extremes of heat and cold, and, in many instances, a lack of potable water.

General James Carleton, who was directing the Apache Expedition from the comfort of his Santa ·Fe headquarters many hundreds of miles away, had a grand vision of quickly subjugating the Apaches. With this as his primary aim, he expected the field units to be highly mobile and decreed that soldiers could carry no food other than meat, bread, sugar, coffee, and salt. He allowed them only one blanket apiece for bedding, saying, "To be encumbered with more is not to find Indians."[6] Some of the scouts lasted up to thirty days, and this spartan regime, combined with the necessity to drink any water which could be found, even brackish, affected the men's health.

Smith Simpson's first Indian scout, undertaken only ten days after the company's arrival at the site of Fort Goodwin, must have convinced him that a jinx controlled his fate when it came to Indian-fighting. The command was moving forward through Apache country in the Pinal Mountains when they were ambushed. Gunfire from the hidden and armed Indians rang out and Simpson was shot just below the ankle, this time on his left leg. The ball splintered and four fragments entered his leg, injuring the Achilles tendon which resulted in permanent partial paralysis and loss of sensation in the leg and foot.

In spite of his wound, Simpson was determined to continue with the expedition. He even requested permission to lead his men on one difficult and dangerous sixteen-day foray after the major in command had decided to leave him behind in camp because of his injury. Simpson was successful in his bid to go.

Several days into the scout, the force employed a strategy it was hoped would surprise the Indians. The men were ordered to blacken their gun barrels with soot to avoid any reflection and, after dark, they began a rapid march toward the Indian villages. The terrain was extremely rough, the night black, and the distance further than expected. In addition, the guides lost their way several times. It was fourteen hours later before the fatigued volunteers finally reached an Apache *rancheria*, on Pinal Creek near the Rio Salinas, at noon. The Indians, however, anticipating the soldier's arrival, had removed their belongings and themselves out of reach on some high rocky ridges bordering the creek. From the safety of the heights they jeered and taunted the soldiers below who, greatly embarrassed, knew it would be fruitless to attempt to reach their quarry.[7]

In the days that followed a number of other incidents occurred, but, at its conclusion, the entire Pinal Creek campaign had taken more than twenty days, the volunteers had covered more than two-hundred-fifty miles, and the net result had been: ten Indians killed, two Apaches captured, twenty acres of Indian corn destroyed, some fields of pumpkins and beans leveled, and a few wickiups burned. General Carleton's dream of easily vanquishing the Arizona Apaches was beginning to ravel at the edges.

## A Ghostly Tale

Even though Captain Simpson's troops ranged the countryside on other Indian scouts and escorted military trains and messengers through the hostile Apache country, a good part of their time was spent in constructing Fort Goodwin. Timber had to be cut in the mountains and hauled down, adobe bricks made, corrals, quarters, and warehouses built, animals cared for, gardens planted, water hauled, firewood gathered and myriad other tasks performed.

Surprisingly, Smith Simpson's main concern for his men's welfare centered not so much on the Indian enemy as upon the Army's inability to supply his command with adequate provisions because of its great isolation. In spite of the hazardous conditions, none of Simpson's volunteers died as a result of field operations or accidents during their three years of service. But disease, mainly from dietary insufficiencies, took its toll. Seven men died during the life of the company and five, or the vast majority, succumbed to scurvy at Fort Goodwin.

The first two years the unit was at Fort Goodwin groups of Pinal and Coyotero Indians, elsewhere along the supply route, managed to practically cut off deliveries to the outpost. At one point the major in command reported that there had been no grain at the camp in over five months and the men, who also lacked any fresh vegetables, soon suffered terribly from scurvy and other related diseases. Some of the unfortunate soldiers became very ill, bleeding from the mouth and vomiting, racked by recurrent bouts of diarrhea, and losing all their teeth. Even the horses and mules at the post became so emaciated from lack of fodder and grain that many died and the others became unfit for active service. The desperate men attempted to put in gardens during the Spring but were thwarted by late freezes and pests. As one man put it, "The army worm destroys everything as soon as it comes up."[8]

In spite of all the hardships, Captain Simpson's company completed its mission and many Apaches in the area offered to surrender. When their enlistments were up in 1866, the company was disbanded and Simpson returned to Taos. Within a short time he was ardently courting a local beauty, *Señorita* Josefa Valdez, a member of one of the oldest families in town.

Josefa, described as "very tiny, with big coal-black eloquent eyes, silky black hair, a perfect lady of dignity," soon accepted Smith Simpson's proposal and the two recited their wedding vows before the priest in the adobe church in Taos. The happy bridegroom purchased an already-standing adobe home, parts of which had been built in the 1820's.

Soon the babies began coming and, as his family enlarged, Simpson added to the house. One of his seven children later recalled idyllic summer evenings when her father, home from his many lengthy business travels, would sit in the yard with his wife and watch the sunset while the children played nearby on buffalo robes.

The Simpson family became one of the most prominent in the scenic town. Simpson raised stock, farmed, and was engaged in the land-grant business, real estate loans, and various other activities. He was widely known as a genial and pleasant man who was always courteous to strangers and always had a place at his table for the hungry or an unexpected guest. This kindly, generous disposition is also attributed to his ghost, a characteristic always mentioned with affection by those who believe in the sightings.

Smith Simpson's long friendship with Kit Carson was a close one. Carson's last words were, "Tell Simpson and Tom Boggs that I wish to be buried at Taos."[9] The great frontiersman's wishes were carried out. Simpson personally spearheaded the effort to erect Carson's headstone, which was supplied by the Santa Fe GAR post. For years the Simpson family kept Carson's grave decorated with beautiful flowers whenever possible.

Smith Simpson outlived his old friends, succumbing in 1916, less than a month before his eighty-third birthday. For more than fifty years he was able to see Old Glory proudly flying night and day in the Taos Plaza, a tribute to his actions. Shortly before his death he said, "I am the only one left, but the flag is still there."[10]

After Simpson's death his home was purchased by an artist and enlarged. Eventually it became a cultural center for the community. Stories about Captain Simpson's ghost at the

# A Ghostly Tale

(*above*) Smith Simpson never forgot his close friend, Kit Carson, and is seen here placing flowers on Carson's grave around the turn of the century.

(*below*) Kit Carson's dying wish was carried out when his body was brought to Taos for burial. Smith Simpson spearheaded a drive to have the GAR supply a headstone for his old comrade. (Author's Collection)

Foundation can still be heard in Taos today. Librarians working alone at night have sworn they often sensed a "presence" nearby, and many unexplained incidents have been attributed to Simpson, who is viewed as a mischievous spectral prankster. Should a book fall from a shelf in an unoccupied room, the lights flicker without apparent reason, or an important paper be misplaced, the inevitable comment is, "The Captain must have done it."

Endnotes:

[1] Dorothy Kethler, *History of the Harwood Foundation* (MS, Harwood Foundation, Taos), p. 2.

[2] *An Illustrated History of New Mexico* (Chicago: Lewis Publishing Company, 1895), p. 610.

[3] Ibid. Also, Smith H. Simpson pension records, National Archives, Washington, D.C.

[4] Jacqueline Dorgan Meketa, *Legacy of Honor* (Albuquerque: University of New Mexico Press, 1986), p. 100.

[5] Ibid.

[6] Brig. Gen. James Carleton, General Order No. 12, Headquarters, Department of New Mexico, Santa Fe, May 1, 1864, Arrott Collection, Highlands University, Las Vegas, NM.

[7] Charles and Jacqueline Meketa, *One Blanket and Ten Days Rations* (Globe, AZ: Southwest Parks and Monuments Assn., 1980), p. 51-55.

[8] *Santa Fe Weekly Gazette*, April 22, 1865.

[9] *An Illustrated History of New Mexico*, p. 611.

[10] *History of the Harwood Foundation*, p. 1.

## My Mother Is A Murderess!

Excitement and anticipation ran high among the curious in Silver City, New Mexico, in mid-December, 1886. They couldn't wait to attend the murder trial of 'Bronco Sue' Yonkers, scheduled for a district court hearing beginning on Wednesday.[1] After all, wild rumors about the woman's past were circulating throughout town. In fact, her lawyers had won a change of venue from Socorro, New Mexico, where the crime occurred, because the rampant gossip, they contended, would prevent a fair trial for their client there. But the most shocking fact was that the woman's own son was to be the principal witness against her!

Here was a woman reputed to have had a rousing career filled with enough adventures to titillate the most avid seeker of second-hand thrills. She was said to have led a dissolute life in the past, to have been involved in various crimes, and to have had relationships with a number of men, many of whom died before they had time to turn gray. Therefore, the local busybodies were anticipating a "painted hussy," a glamorous but sinful lady of voluptuous curves, painted cheeks, and high-piled hair.

# My Mother Is A Murderess!

The imposing Silver City courthouse as it looked when Susan Yonkers apparently hornswoggled a jury once again.
(Museum of New Mexico)

Instead, when they pushed into the crowded courtroom on the appointed day, they found, much to their disappointment, a forty-five year old gray-haired female who looked anything but decadent.

The *Silver City Enterprise* described Sue as follows: "From her appearance she was evidently used to a life of rough battling with the world; stern looking, tall, rather slender, with the head of a man, self-possessed, respectable looking, but unattractive."[2]

The newspaper also printed a biographical sketch of the accused, which it prefaced with a statement implying the editors would not vouch for its authenticity, and for which no source was given. According to the story, the defendant was originally named Susan Warfield and, as a child, accompanied her parents from Wales to Nevada. There she grew up to be a daring horsewoman, a deadly shot, the darling of a mining camp, and was eventually wooed and won by Thomas D. Raper with whom she had two sons.

As the tale goes, shortly thereafter hostile Indians raided the mining camp. Susan's brother was shot, and her husband wounded. The girl was supposed to have strapped her suffering husband to a horse, killed two Indians, and then carried her man to safety. However, this was apparently only a story circulated to enhance Sue's reputation.

After the trial a gentleman appeared at the local newspaper office and said he had known Susan Warfield when she was a "winsome frontier girl and honored young wife, ere the days of her wild career began."[3] He stated "...the Indian fight you spoke of did not take place. Her brother was killed but the wound her husband got was made by his own gun while trying to draw the weapon from the wagon when Indians were approaching." He also stated that Sue was only fifteen years old at the time of her marriage to Raper, who owned both the Yankie Mine at Downieville, California, and twelve thousand dollars. After Sue's high living depleted all his assets, she separated from her husband and became a terrible "hustler," living with cattle thieves and "insulting and laughing at the judge whenever taken into court," according to the witness. Other stories from the area claim that shortly after Susan and Thomas separated, she made a trek to California with an unnamed "gallant scout." Upon their return, the pair was accused of stealing jewelry and other articles.[4]

It was also bandied about that on one occasion, when she and a partner in crime were fleeing from a deputy sheriff, her escort sustained a wound. Susan gave him her horse, which was the strongest and fastest, and then held the deputy at bay with a revolver until the injured man made his escape. She was also known to be an associate of one Colonel Robert Payne, who was engaged in horse stealing in the Humbolt Valley.

Tired of life in Nevada, Susan eventually went from Elko to Colorado, and for a time lived in Pueblo under the name of Susan Stone. She then acquired a stage line which ran between

## My Mother Is A Murderess!

Conejos and San Antonio, Colorado. In 1882, she married Jack Yonkers, formerly of Independence, Arkansas, and moved to northern New Mexico, where she kept a saloon in the town of Wallace.[5] After several moves the two decided to try their luck in Lincoln county, which, at that time, had gained renown as the site of the "Lincoln County War," featuring the exploits of Billy the Kid.

While en route they camped in an empty cabin, and before long a yellow flag was hung out and no one ventured near the place.[6] Several weeks later Susan Yonkers left the cabin, saying that her husband had died of smallpox and she had dug his grave and buried him.

But she did not travel on alone. By a most felicitous, but suspicious stroke of luck, Susan found a farmer named Robert Black living nearby who decided to leave his place and accompany her to Lincoln County. In spite of her plainness, Susan was able to attract handsome fellows. Black was described as six feet tall, weighing about 175 pounds, fine looking, and wearing a heavy black beard.[7] For a while Susan lived in Lincoln County with Black and her sons, who had preceded her there from Colorado. Then wanderlust hit again and she went westward to the mining town of Soccoro, New Mexico, where she began keeping a boarding house and her "friend," Robert Black, ran a profitable saloon. On occasions, Sue presided over the bar and, at other times, dealt "stud" to the watering hole's clientele.

One journalist reported that on a Saturday night in August, 1884, the sheriff took possession of the saloon and it was then that Black was heard angrily demanding that Mrs. Yonkers return his money to him. Instead, she called the city marshal and had the irate and intoxicated man taken away stating, at the time, that if he returned she would kill him.

Another reporter had a different version: the two lovebirds had made a good sum of money with the saloon, every cent was saved, and, in due time a ranch was purchased. He wrote that the ranch was later sold for cash and the profits banked in an account to which Sue had access. Shortly thereafter the two had a falling out and Sue swore out a warrant and had her common-law husband thrown into the hoosegow.[8]

*(above)* Even though this Socorro saloon photo is from the same era, it cannot be determined whether or not it was the one run by Sue's "friend," Robert Black. (Author's Collection) *(below)* Susan Yonker's attorney feared the citizens of early Socorro, seen below, would not be impartial in judging his client and requested her murder case be moved out of town. (Socorro Historical Society)

## My Mother Is A Murderess!

Whatever the circumstances, on Sunday, August 24, 1884, Black was out of jail and apparently spent the day drinking. He returned home about five in the afternoon and was heard once again protesting vehemently about having been turned out of the boarding house and angrily demanding the return of his money. At this point, according to a newspaper account,"...Mrs. Yonkers went down town, bought a pistol, lured a colored man to go to another place after cartridges, and returned home. Soon after two shots were fired in quick succession. She at once emerged from the house and went to the sheriff's office and surrendered herself, saying she had shot Black in self-defense."[9] Once again 'Bronco Sue' was without a man.

She was taken before a justice of the peace. Her attorney entered a plea of self defense; the prosecution had no lawyer; and soon the murder charge was dismissed.

Shortly thereafter, the ever-on-the-move Susan left town and went to Doña Ana County in the southern part of the territory. The travel dust hardly had time to settle before Sue was trotting down the aisle again. This time she married a gentleman named Charles Dawson. Alas, poor Charlie! Before the marital bed had time to get warm this husband was shot to death, under controversial circumstances, by J. H. Good. Once again Sue donned her widow's weeds.[10]

The shooting took place at La Luz, a small town in southern New Mexico, which was first settled in the early 1700s. Trouble had been brewing between Dawson and Good for some months. On one occasion Good accused Dawson of writing to his wife and telling her that he had been keeping a mistress. Dawson denied the charge, and several times asked for an amicable settlement of their differences.

One Tuesday in early December, 1885, Good requested a meeting and Dawson agreed. Each man took along several cohorts. When Dawson left the house he was accompanied by Sue's son, William Raper, and another young man. As soon as they departed, Sue snatched up a Winchester rifle and followed them saying that if there was any trouble she would be there; if not, she would keep the rifle hidden. According to her later testimony, her motive seemed to be to protect "her boy," and not her husband.

The two armed groups approached within several yards of each other and in moments half a dozen shots rang out. Dawson slumped to the ground dead, with three of Good's bullets in him. At a preliminary hearing, Sue dramatically testified that when she saw her fallen husband she "ran and held Dawson in her arms where he died."[11]

Shortly after the shooting Good was taken before a justice of the peace and acquitted of any charges. But within days Sue sent her son, William, to Las Cruces to sign a complaint. As a result, Good and another man were bound over for trial after a three day preliminary hearing filled with conflicting testimony. However, there were other results which Sue had not anticipated. The irate Good filed counter charges against William for assault with an attempt to kill, and William was bound over with bail set at five hundred dollars cash.

Eventually, William was tried and acquitted on the charges, but not before his mother had paid a lawyer five hundred dollars to defend him and had put up bond on his behalf. This apparent concern and closeness between mother and son were to make later events all the more surprising and distasteful to the courtroom spectators when Sue was on trial for Black's murder.

In early 1886, when Good was brought to trial, Sue returned to Las Cruces to appear as one of the principal witnesses against him. It was then that she was arrested on an indictment stemming from the shooting of Black in Socorro two years earlier.

Rumors immediately began to fly that Susan's arrest was a conspiracy to prevent her testimony against Good. But the district attorney denied the allegations, saying that Socorro citizens merely felt that the prior district attorney had been remiss in not attending to the matter a year or two earlier. It also seemed that her son, William Raper, had voluntarily appeared before the Socorro grand jury and revealed startling information which incriminated both his mother and his brother, Joseph. Whether

## My Mother Is A Murderess!

or not there was any intrigue afoot to benefit him, Good was eventually acquitted on the grounds of self-defense.

After Susan Yonkers was arrested in Las Cruces and brought back to Socorro, the town's newspapers began to print articles about her scandalous earlier life and activities. There was also the matter of a little charge that she had supplied steel rods from her corset to help her son, Joseph, and some other prisoners break out of jail. This adverse publicity caused her attorneys, P. Hamilton and Col. A. J. Fountain, to procure the change of venue which resulted in the trial being held in Silver City.[12]

This, then, was the path through life which brought Susan Yonkers to Silver City and the courthouse shortly before Christmas, 1886. It is highly probable that Susan was not terribly apprehensive about the trial and its outcome, considering her previous abundant success in manipulating both men and the legal system to her advantage. She certainly had escaped unscathed from some very sticky situations. Much more unsettling must have been the knowledge that her first born had turned against her.

As the trial progressed, the audience in the packed courtroom heard the prosecutor aver that Black's murder had been nothing more than a conspiracy by Susan to obtain Black's money and property, and that she had plotted to carry out the crime in such a way that no eye witnesses would be present.

In spite of some very damaging testimony against the accused, the newspaper reporter and most of the town's citizens appeared to be much more shocked by, and interested in, the twenty-three year old son, William Raper, who, as the newspaper put it, "was base enough to try to procure the conviction of his mother and brother," than in Susan herself. While admitting that Susan had hardly raised her sons in an exemplary atmosphere, the newspaper's editors seemed horrified at the thought of any son accusing "the woman who gave him birth," no matter what she might have done.

William Raper testified that his mother originally proposed a plan to entice Black to her bed and have her other son,

Joseph, kill him. The motive was to obtain the ranch and the many cattle and horses Black owned. William said the family all agreed upon the scheme, which even included such details as having William caring for the ranch and livestock after Black's death while the mother arranged for, and assisted in, the defense of her son, Joseph, when he was accused of the murder.

William testified, however, that his mother killed Black herself, earlier than planned, because he had threatened to send her and Joseph to jail for stealing some of his horses and beef and selling them at Fort Stanton. William said he had even helped his mother kill some of the beeves. William also testified that his mother had told him she placed an axe near Black's dead body in order to create an appearance that her life had been in danger when she shot him.

The defense attorney immediately attacked William's character, demanding to know if he was testifying against his mother in order to have her convicted so, he himself could obtain the livestock and property the family controlled. William denied any such motive. He said he did not desire to see his mother hung, and stated that he had helped to procure a bond for her when she was in custody in Socorro by pledging seven thousand dollars worth of cattle and horses. The defense attorney then managed to get William to admit that he had since sold one of the horses. The attorney also brought up several other little acts he hoped would discredit the son's character.

During the entire proceedings, Susan Yonkers frequently placed her handkerchief to her eyes and, when she was testifying, a few tears wet her cheeks. Shortly thereafter, however, when another witness was on the stand, audible snickers were heard emanating from behind her handkerchief when an amusing remark was made.

While on the stand Susan testified that the day of the shooting Black called her vile names, threw a goblet which struck her on the shoulder, and then rushed to one corner of the room, picked up the axe and started toward her in a threatening manner. She said she ran and got a .38 caliber revolver, which

## My Mother Is A Murderess!

just happened to be lying on the mantelpiece in the front room, and aimed and shot when she believed her life was in danger.

If Sue's story was true, either she was lucky or an excellent shot, because the bullet passed through Black's left arm and pierced his heart. He expired almost immediately.

When asked about the alleged conversations with William regarding a plan to murder Black, Susan turned on the tears and replied she did not wish to prove her son a perjurer, but that she had never proposed to commit a murder, or admitted to one.

The defense then called upon a Black man who said he had heard the shattering of a glass and the noise of the shooting as he happened to be passing by. Whether or not this was the same gentleman who had earlier purchased the cartridges as a favor for Sue apparently was not established. His testimony was taken, by the jury, as corroboration of Susan's testimony. The defense submitted no other evidence.

On the afternoon of the second day the case went to the jury. In just a few minutes, after only two ballots, a verdict of not guilty was rendered.

If the newspaper account is to be believed, Susan Yonker's guilt or innocence appeared to be of little concern to either the citizens or the jury. The issue in question seemed to be a son's unconditional loyalty and devotion to his mother, no matter what the circumstances.

The newspaper editorialized, "Certainly no one expected that a son reared as he had been should be governed by all the finer impulses, for oranges cannot be made to grow on sagebrush; but from the mouths of men only expressions of scorn could be heard for this depraved young man—a self-confessed scoundrel, whose reputation is sworn to be bad where he has lived. Granting his story was true in every particular in reference to acts of his mother, those who believed it believed him baser than she, and many who heard his testimony declared him to be the one who should be hung."[13]

In reference to the not guilty verdict, the reporter wrote: "the result had been anticipated generally, for the only testimony showing a guilty intention was given by Mrs. Yonker's son. A jury could scarcely be had in America that would convict a yellow dog of the larceny of a beef bone upon the accusation of so depraved a witness as a son must be who would have the woman hanged who gave him birth."[14]

So 'Bronco Sue' was free once again. What further adventures she might have had are unknown. But if her prior history was any indication, Sue would do plenty more traveling and link up with plenty more men. It is to be hoped that they were not as prone to sudden death as their predecessors.

Endnotes:

[1] While the December 17, 1886, *Silver City Enterprise* used the nickname 'Bronco Sue' in an article on the murder trial, two years earlier the *Albuquerque Evening Democrat* of August 25, 1884, had dubbed her 'Buckskin Sue' when reporting the murder in Socorro.

[2] *Silver City Enterprise*, New Mexico Territory, December 17, 1886.

[3] Ibid., December 24, 1886.

[4] Some of this information apparently came from a Judge Keeny, who was the magistrate for one of Susan's trials in Nevada and was later serving in Socorro, New Mexico, when she was accused of murder there. See *Silver City Enterprise*, December 17, 1886.

[5] There were two towns named Wallace in New Mexico. It has not been determined if Sue was living in the one between Albuquerque and Santa Fe or the one in northeastern New Mexico in Colfax County. The latter was named for General Lew Wallace, New Mexico Territorial Governor from 1878 to 1881, and author of the novel, *Ben Hur*.

[6] The yellow flag signaled pestilence and, if something underhanded was going on, would be an effective way to keep unwanted visitors away.

[7] *Albuquerque Evening Democrat*, August 25, 1884.

[8] The differing versions were in the *Albuquerque Evening Democrat* and the *Silver City Enterprise* issues already cited.

[9] *Silver City Enterprise*, December 17, 1886.

[10] Again there is a discrepancy in the facts as reported by several newspapers. The *Rio Grande Republican* issues of December 12 and December 19, 1885, published in Las Cruces, New Mexico, both refer to the man has J. H. Good. The *Silver City Enterprise* issue of December 17, 1886, reported the man's name as Frank Goode. It is probable that the *Republican's* information is correct since it was closer to the shooting, both geographically and chronologically.

## My Mother Is A Murderess!

[11] *Rio Grande Republican*, December 19, 1885.

[12] Susan Yonkers had hired one of the most prestigious attorneys in southern New Mexico in the person of A. J. Fountain. A prominent man with great political clout, he was known to be both ambitious and vain. In 1896, his name would enter the annals of New Mexico history when he and his young son were murdered near the White Sands, while returning from a trip. The mystery regarding the circumstances of their deaths was never solved, resulting in an unhappy celebrity which insured Fountain a sort of dubious fame.

[13] *Silver City Enterprise*, December 17, 1886.

[14] Ibid.

## Mystery Death in the Palace

It was a peaceful Sunday morning in June, 1869, and the church bells at the cathedral in Santa Fe were pealing for early Mass, awakening both sinners and the faithful. But the young servant girl hurrying down the hallway in the adobe Palace of the Governors had risen more than an hour before. As always, she had made a fire and cooked breakfast for the Colonel. Now, following her usual routine, she entered his bedroom to awaken him so he could eat and she could make his bed.

Moments later the young woman's horrified screams tore the morning quiet. On the floor, lying in a pool of blood, was the dead body of Colonel James L. Collins, one of the longest-residing and most eminent citizens of the New Mexico Territory. Shock turned her cold, then she whirled and ran, stumbling and crying, out of the building and through the streets to the nearby home of the colonel's daughter, Mrs. James M. Edgar.

By the time the lamenting daughter and her husband rushed to the scene, the news had begun to spread through Santa Fe

## Mystery Death

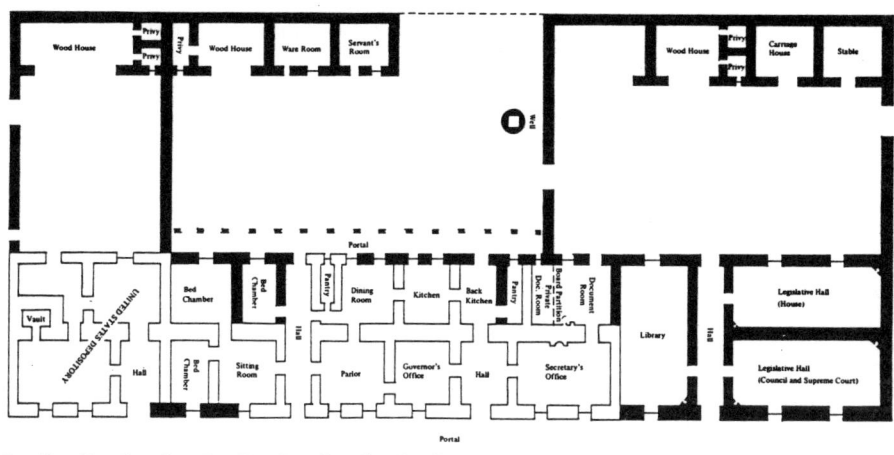

Just six months before James L. Collins' mysterious death, this floor plan of the Palace was sent to the secretary of the treasury. The U.S. Depository, where the body was found, is at lower left. (National Archives)

like a prairie fire. Within a few minutes large numbers of excited people assembled at the scene of the tragedy. Most expressed outrage that this greatly esteemed elderly man had been murdered. For the past three years, this man had held the position of United States Depositary, responsible for safeguarding all the Federal monies in the city.

Indignation ran high that such a bold and nefarious act could have occurred and that the brave old gentleman, known to almost every resident by sight, should have perished in the course of his duty of protecting the public funds. In addition, there was the irony of the timing of the tragedy. It was well known that the following morning, Monday, Colonel Collins had been scheduled to turn over the Depository to his successor, a Captain E. W. Little.

On the day following the event, citizens were able to imagine the death scene from a description published in the local newspaper:

# From Martyrs to Murderers

> ...Upon entering the room the diabolical work of the assassins and robbers was presented to view. The dead body of Col. Collins lay upon the floor in a pool of coagulated blood with a bullet hole through the heart, and over the floor were scattered various sealed packages of fractional currency and sundry piles of the same in small quantities, while the money vault and iron safe showed that they had been broken open and all the bills of large denominations extracted and carried away. The amount of these it is believed is probably not less that $100,000.[1]

Three official acts now took place. Even as the body was being removed a committee of federal officials inventoried the public monies remaining in the Depository and informally gave Captain Little possession of the funds that were left. In addition, a list of the serial numbers of quite a few newly-arrived and as yet undistributed legal tender (twenty dollar notes) was published in the next day's newspaper. Several days later, H. H. Heath, the Territorial Secretary, issued a proclamation offering a "large reward," of some unspecified amount, for "the discovery and arrest of the perpetrators of this diabolical murder and robbery."[2]

Word was also sent immediately to Albuquerque because Collins was one of the best known men in the Territory. In 1826, twenty years before New Mexico became part of the United States, he had set off from Missouri to cross the great plains with wagons of goods to trade in Santa Fe and Chihuahua, thus becoming one of the first Americans to arrive in the area. After service in the Mexican-American War he enjoyed a long and important career in Santa Fe, which included many diverse activities.

He was involved in exploration of wilderness areas and the establishment of the *Santa Fe Weekly Gazette*, which he published for six years. He was also appointed the Territory's Superintendent of Indian Affairs by President Buchanan, and reappointed by Abraham Lincoln.

## Mystery Death

The southwest corner of the plaza in Santa Fe in 1855. James Collins, whose portrait has never been discovered, could well be one of the men posed in front of the Exchange Hotel, a favorite gathering place for Santa Fe's important men.
(Museum of New Mexico)

During the Civil War, when Sibley's army of Texans had penetrated New Mexico and was marching toward Fort Union, Collins helped guide Union soldiers to the Texans' hidden supply train, which was then destroyed, assuring the defeat of the invaders.

Such prominence guaranteed that all Santa Fe and, indeed, the Territory, would be buzzing with rumor and conjecture. Several days later the local newspaper dedicated much space to the story, as well as an effusive eulogy and biography of Colonel Collins.

The newspaper reported that the investigation had shown the robbers had entered the *placita* at the rear and then forced the back door of the office open with iron bars, thus gaining access to the front room which housed both an iron safe and a vault for storing the government monies. With a figurative shake of its editorial head, the newspaper said, "The vault was supposed to be strongly constructed and the mechanism of the door so perfect that it would be burglar proof. These rascals, however, being masters of their profession showed that nothing is impossible with their fraternity."[3]

The writer then proceeded to reconstruct the crime through conjecture and in florid prose. The article continued:

> They [the robbers], beyond doubt, went to work immediately after having entered the office to search for the keys to the door of the vault. In all probability the first effort in this direction was to open the iron safe in expectation of finding them there. The door of that safe was opened without much difficulty, it being only fastened with a padlock which was forced with a long, strong, steel bar used for closing the window shutters on the inside. Whether the keys, of which they finally possessed themselves, were found or not will probably forever remain a mystery as it is at the present time. The presumption is that Col. Collins, who was alone in the office, and who had retired, was aroused by their operations, got up, lighted a candle, put on his slippers, took a revolver and light in hand, and proceeded through the hall to the office to see what was being done. The robbers were, unfortunately, but too ready for him. All the indications show that as soon as he opened the door two shots were fired at him; one missing and the other, with most murderous effect, passing through the heart, coming out of the back about two inches lower than it entered the breast. Death must have been produced almost instantaneously as would be indicated by the blood on the floor and the position of the body—a ghastly, sickening sight which brought tears to the eyes of men who are unused to weep.
>
> Once in possession of the keys, and the only obstacle to their nefarious designs being, by their bloody hands, transferred from time to eternity, the murderers proceeded with their robbery. The condition in which the door of the vault was found in the morning showed that they perfectly understood the

construction of the burglar proof lock with which they had to deal, and they dealt with it accordingly.

They expertly opened the door of the vault and without much more difficulty had access to a large portion of the object of their desires. Much of the money which thus became within their control was in fractional currency, which they carried out of the vault, examined by opening the wrappers and left it promiscuously scattered about—on the counter, on chairs, on the tables, and on the floor. The larger bills were stolen and amounted, in the aggregate, as near as could be estimated, to about one hundred thousand dollars.

The murderers and robbers left the building without disturbance, so far as is known, leaving their victim, the noblest work of God, one honest man weltering in his blood, and carrying with them their booty—the reward of murder the most atrocious, and robbery the most daring.

Thus far all was successful. The murdered man could tell no tales. The notes were stolen, and to all appearances, in the safe possession of those who had dared and done so much to obtain them. But the success did not prove so complete. On Tuesday morning after the deed was committed a large portion of the notes was found in an unoccupied building, at the north end of the city, known as the city brewery.[4] The notes were tied up in packages of ten thousand dollars each with the exception of one which contained a smaller sum. The total amount recovered was sixty five thousand six hundred dollars and was placed in custody of the U. S. Depositary, E. W. Little, to await orders of the proper authorities of the United States.

The amount of money, therefore, yet in the hands of the robbers is not so very large. This, however, should not be any reason for relaxing vigilance in their apprehension. The great crime of the transaction remains to be punished by the law, and never will be atoned for until the criminals hear pronounced upon them on the day of Judgment the awful sentence, "Depart from Me and prepare for the Devil and his angels."[5]

# From Martyrs to Murderers

## A PROCLAMATION!
### GREAT REWARD.

WHEREAS, On last Saturday night, the 5th instant, the United States Depository in this city was robbed by parties unknown, and a large amount of public money taken therefrom, and Col. JAMES L. COLLINS, the United States Depositary, murdered.

Now, BE IT KNOWN, That, in the absence of the Governor from the Capitol, I hereby issue this proclamation, earnestly requesting all good citizens throughout this Territory and elsewhere, and the military authorities likewise, to assist in the discovery and arrest of the perpetrators of this diabolical murder and robbery.

No fixed reward can now be offered, but assurance is hereby given that A LARGE REWARD will be paid by the Government to any person who will either secure the treasure lost, or discover the authors of these crimes, or give such certain information as will lead to their apprehension.

The delivery of any or all of the perpetrators of these crimes at any Military Post in New Mexico, will be regarded as a delivery to the Government.

Santa Fé, June 6, 1869.

H. H. HEATH,
Secretary New Mexico.

## UNA PROCLAMA.
### GRANDE RECOMPENSA!

Por cuanto, la noche del sabado pasado dia 5 del corriente, la oficina del Depositario de los Estados Unidos en esta ciudad, ha sido robado por personas desconocidas, las cuales han tomado una grande suma del dinero publico, dando por consecuencia el asesinato del coronel Santiago L. Collins, depositario de los Estados Unidos. Con pleno conocimiento de la triste desgracia, y estando el Gobernador ausente de esta capital, me veo obligado a poner esta proclamacion lo mas pronto posible, suplicando a todo buen ciudadano de este territorio y de cualquier otra parte y a las autoridades militares que ayuden en lo posible para descubrir y arrestar a los perpetradores del robo y del homocidio diabolico que han cometido.

No se fija la recompensa que debe ser pagado, pero si se asegura una grande suma que sera pagada por el gobierno a la persona que descubra a los autores de tan nefandos crimines, o que de alguna informacion segura para la aprehension de ellos.

La entrega de cualquiera o de todos los perpetradores de estos crimines en cualquiera posta militar en Nuevo Mejico, sera considerada entrega al gobierno.

Santa Fe, Junio 6 de 1869.

H. H. HEATH,
Secretario del Territorio.

The reward proclamation, published in the local newspapers, was printed in both Spanish and English for bilingual Santa Fe. (WeeklyNew Mexican, June 8, 1869)

# Mystery Death

Ironically, the hidden money was found on the very morning of Colonel Collins' funeral. It was a large, imposing affair, of the sort usually conducted for social and political leaders of any community. The lamented deceased was borne from the home of his only child, Mrs. James M. Edgar, to Santa Fe's Masonic cemetery escorted by military, federal, and territorial officers, families in carriages, and a crowd of citizens from every class. But already the capital was awash with scandalous rumors. One newspaper reported that even though all sorts of stories about the "unfortunate affair" were floating about Santa Fe, the publication felt that "the cause of justice would not be subserved by repeating them" and it would refrain from doing so.[6]

Here was a mystery of magnificent proportions; one that fairly screamed out for a Sherlock Holmes. But alas, though the questions were many, the answers were few. We are left to ponder many incongruities, and the passage of time has eliminated any chance of determining facts which could push aside the veil over the face of the mystery.

A number of possibilities immediately come to mind upon learning of the story. The first, of course, is that the event was indeed what it was reported to be—a murder and robbery. The second is that Colonel Collins had embezzled the approximately thirty five thousand dollars which was never recovered and, knowing an accounting would be necessary within a day, set up an elaborate "robbery scenario" to save his good name and then committed suicide. A third possibility also exists—that James Edgar, the son-in-law, committed the crime. Each theory has possibilities.

The first interpretation of events became the official version even though no culprits were ever apprehended, the balance of the money never turned up, and rumors and speculation continued for years to come. Within days of this spectacular event, after the portion of the missing money was found in Santa Fe, Territorial newspapers suddenly dropped all mention of the affair from their pages.

Also, in a report accompanying an 1874 House of Representatives bill to relieve the men acting as Collins' sureties of the necessity of repaying the still-missing money to the Federal government, the murder-robbery explanation was deemed correct. It was, of course, in the interest of the men who had bonded Collins to have this conclusion reached, since they were all men of some importance and influence.[7] The Congressional committee stated they were satisfied, from the evidence, that Collins had been an excellent officer, had always been known for his integrity, patriotism, and courage and that, as an elderly man, he had lived a simple life of good habits and exhibited no questionable traits.

The second theory, that of a suicide to cover up a monetary discrepancy, presumably is the one which occurred to a number of other people at the time although this was not publicized in print. Many years later an Albuquerque newspaper carried a series of articles in which a former acquaintance of Colonel Collins stated that the colonel had indeed committed suicide.[8] But many questions remain. Had the colonel's gun, found beside his body, been fired twice? Was it of the same caliber as the bullet which killed him? Were there any powder burns on his clothing which would show that the gun was held against his chest when it was discharged, as a suicide might do to assure a quick and painless death? Did the locks, safe, and vault show few or no signs of the kind of crude, forceful entry strong and unskilled thugs would carry out, as the newspaper reports seemed to imply, or did they appear to have been opened by someone with keys and easy access? Then there was the inventory of the Depository assets which was reportedly done several days *before* Collins' death in preparation to turning the funds over to Mr. Little. A Congressional report stated that Collins, "with James M. Edgar, his clerk, and John T. Russell, now deceased, a former clerk, had thoroughly examined his books, counted the moneys on hand, and all were found correct."[9] Was all the money there or did Collins, possibly in collusion with his son-in-law, manage to falsify the records?

Finally, there is the inescapable suspicion that Mr. Edgar was involved in the whole matter, either as perpetrator or accomplice. Collins had only one child, his daughter, and her

## Mystery Death

husband was employed as his clerk. If the colonel had a weakness, such as gambling or making unwise investments, it would seem that Edgar would be aware of the problem or at least suspect it, since the two men had such extremely close ties, both professional and familial.

If, on the other hand, Edgar had a desperate need for the money because of problems generated by his own lifestyle, such information never became part of the public record since no suspicion seemed to fall on him. However, if one wished to speculate about all the possibilities, it is true that Edgar would have been totally familiar with all the conditions at the Depository, and possibly would no longer have been employed there once the colonel was replaced. Then, too, there is the question of why the Albuquerque newspaper reported that the recovered funds were found "in the privy of an unoccupied house belonging to Mr. J. M. Edgar, as we were informed by a party from the Capitol last evening."[10] Even if the report was not true, some suspicions must have generated such a story. We are also left to wonder if the recovered bills consisted, at least partially, of those whose serial numbers had been published, making them useless locally.

Regardless of whether James Edgar was in any way involved in the death of his father-in-law or not, he and his wife were dealt another bitter blow when they received word of "the cruel murder" of their son less than three months after his grandfather's death.[11]

The local newspaper ran a copy of a letter the family received from a man writing from the Mimbres River area in southwestern New Mexico. He informed them that their son James C. had been murdered near that spot by some Texans with whom he had been traveling. The young man's body was not discovered until several days after a large cattle drove, headed for California, and two of its employees, who were suspected of the deed, had left the area.

With that last irony, the story seems to end. The mystery of James L. Collins' death has remained unsolved. To this day a cloud of suspicion hovers over his memory, leaving a rather bizarre end to a long and illustrious public career.

# From Martyrs to Murderers

Endnotes:

[1] *Weekly New Mexican*, June 8, 1869.

[2] Ibid., June 15, 1869.

[3] *Santa Fe Weekly Gazette*, June 12, 1869.

[4] In a conflicting report, printed the day before the previous *Gazette* account, the *Semi-Weekly Review* in Albuquerque reported on June 11, 1869, that $65,000 of the stolen money was recovered in the privy of an unoccupied house belonging to Mr. J. M. Edgar, who, of course, was Colonel Collins' son-in-law and clerk.

[5] *Santa Fe Weekly Gazette*, June 12, 1869.

[6] *Semi-Weekly Review*, June 11, 1869.

[7] Among those who had acted as sureties were John Sebrie Watts, a lawyer who had been an elected Delegate to Congress from New Mexico and also served as an Associate Justice and then Chief Justice of the Territorial Supreme Court. Another was William W. Mills of El Paso, Texas, a prominent merchant who held sway as a political boss in that area for years. A judgment against the men for $38,593.35 was rendered in the United States District Court in Santa Fe. They appealed it and the Congressional bill was a successful petition by the men to be relieved of repayment responsibilities.

[8] According to Howard Bryan, in his column "Off the Beaten Path," *Albuquerque Tribune*, March 16, 1972, a former stagecoach driver, Sandy Wardwell, stated in a series of personal recollections in an 1897 issue of the *Albuquerque Weekly News* that Collins had committed suicide and hidden approximately $75,000 in "an outhouse and the old brewery." The motive, according to Wardwell, was Collins' desire to "sacrifice himself to give his daughter a stake and Edward, his son-in-law, did not have the nerve to keep it but went and gave it all away and the good old man died in vain." Wardwell's accuracy, however, could be questionable since, in his other recollections, he appears to enjoy placing himself in the limelight, and perhaps exaggerated his exploits to a degree.

[9] Report No. 104, 43rd Congress, 1st Session, House of Representatives.

[10] *Semi-Weekly Review*, June 11, 1869.

[11] *Santa Fe Weekly Gazette*, September 18, 1869.

# The *Bandido* and the *Señorita*

That Friday was a beautiful March day in 1886 in the little settlement of San Lorenzo, tucked away in mountains in the southwestern corner of New Mexico. The sun was shining and a slight breeze wafted the pristine air through the mountain meadow grass and nearby pines. A winsome fifteen-year-old *señorita,* leaning over the pigsty walls, was busy feeding the family swine, when suddenly she heard the sound of galloping horses bearing down upon her. One startled look showed three male riders approaching rapidly and, screaming with fear, she wheeled and began to run toward the cabin.

Within moments Reyes Alvarez was overtaken, snatched up, and placed upon a horse. As her mother rushed to the door to help her daughter, she was met by a fusillade of fourteen shots from the outlaws's guns. By some extraordinary good fortune, the woman was not hit, but the girl's brother, also hurrying to her aid, was struck in the leg and seriously wounded. Within moments, the whole affair was over and the kidnappers had raced off with their captive.[1]

## From Martyrs to Murderers

Immediately, men residing in the vicinity were aroused and a party of pursuing citizens was soon on the trail. The residents knew that a band of Mexican-American rustlers was camped in the nearby Santa Rita Mountains. But, discretion being the better part of valor, they were ignored until this trio dashed down the Mimbres River, stole two bay horses, and then abducted the girl.

The impromptu posse followed the culprits's trail and before long overtook them. A spirited gun battle ensued. Although the fight continued for some time, the outlaws could not be dislodged because they had cleverly positioned themselves high in the boulders above their pursuers. The posse, after one of the citizens was killed by a bullet, decided to discontinue the fighting at that spot and allow the kidnappers to retreat. The offenders's tracks were subsequently followed over the mountains, but, even though they were marked by blood in some places, and in spite of the efforts of several search parties over the next few days, neither the men nor the girl was found.

The following Tuesday, about ten o'clock at night, a traveler stumbled upon an injured man about a mile north of Silver City, at the junction of two main roads. It was almost an hour before the wounded man could be brought into town. It was then learned that he was Deputy Sheriff Thomas Hall. He had been shot twice, one bullet passing through his body from the right to the left side, and the other shattering his right arm.

The deputy was so weak from loss of blood and exposure that he could barely inform the authorities that he had been shot by a man of Mexican descent whom he did not know. He promised to supply further details about the affair after he had received medical help. He had left town that morning to handle some private business at nearby Pinos Altos (Tall Pines) and was returning when shot, probably just about dark.

In spite of the best surgical efforts of the town's doctor, it soon became apparent the patient was slipping away. Shortly after midnight, as he was attempting to recount the details of his shooting, Tom Hall died.

# The *Bandido* and the *Señorita*

The Georgetown-Silver City stagecoach photographed in Silver City in the 1880s. If Sheriff Hall had taken this transportation instead of his horse, his murder would not have occurred. (Museum of New Mexico)

During the night the horse Hall had been riding wandered back into town without its saddle, indicating to many that whoever did the killing had ridden the horse, then later unsaddled it and turned it loose. As word of the event spread about the community, some Hispanic wood haulers reported that earlier that day, before Hall was shot, they too had been traveling to Silver City along the road from Pinos Altos. They had seen another Hispaño leading a horse upon which a girl or woman was riding and he had been armed with a rifle. It was assumed that Hall must have overtaken this pair at just about the point where the shooting took place.

The immediate conjecture was that the man who had killed Hall must be one of the trio of desperados; that he had been bringing the kidnapped girl into town; and that he had lain in ambush until his victim came into easy range. And, even though the deputy had originally stated he didn't know the man who shot him, other citizens offered the theory that Hall, on overtaking the man, recognized him as one of the band of fugitives, tried to arrest him, and was bested in a gun fight. This flight of fancy was founded on the fact that Hall had fired one shot from his pistol and, based on his wounds, it was surmised that he could not have discharged his weapon after being shot.

At any rate, the town's citizens were outraged over the event. Hall, considered an old-timer in Grant County, where mining booms and busts, as well as Indian troubles, tended to generate a rather fluid population, had lived in Pinos Altos for a number of years before becoming a Silver City deputy sheriff three years earlier. He was considered not only an honest, brave, and competent law man but, tragically, left behind a wife and five small children.

Several days after Deputy Hall's last rites, the truth was revealed. On the evening of the killing a young girl named Reyes Alvarez had appeared at the Silver City home of a Mrs. Fessler and asked for shelter. Terrified that she would be killed by desperate members of the gang that had kidnapped her, she concealed the fact that she had knowledge of the deputy's murder. Finally, after questioning by her hostess and then, by a coroner's jury, she fearfully told her story.

The girl recounted how, after her abduction, she was being brought in toward town on the trail from Pinos Altos by one of her kidnappers, a man named Pilar. She stated they were overtaken by Hall who traveled along with them for some distance and, becoming suspicious, began to question Pilar, asking what his name was, where he lived, etc.

The outlaw replied with lies but as the questioning continued it became more and more difficult to come up with answers. On some pretext he managed to drop behind Hall and, taking deliberate aim, fired at the deputy. This first shot knocked Hall off his horse and, even though seriously wounded, he scrambled to his feet and began to run. Pilar, with cool deliberation, aimed and fired another bullet into the deputy, who fell to the ground, according to the young woman.

## The *Bandido* and the *Señorita*

During the commotion the girl, the unwitting target of Pilar's love—or lust—managed to escape and hide. She stated that the last time she saw Pilar he was mounted upon Hall's horse and endeavoring to catch his own animal. The coroner's jury questioned the girl very closely but were unable to catch her in any contradictory or suspicious statements. In addition, her account of the events matched perfectly all the physical evidence they had previously discovered. Since she was the only eyewitness to Hall's murder, it was decided that she should be kept in town under the protection of the sheriff, at least for the next few days, while a posse was sent out in search of the killer.

The posse was unsuccessful in hunting down Pilar Saiz who was dubbed, by the Anglo residents of Silver City, the leader of the outlaws. Reyes Alvarez soon returned home to help her mother care for her brother, whose wounds had necessitated the amputation of his leg.

About six weeks after Sheriff Hall's demise the *Silver City Enterprise* of April 30, 1886, reported that "a number of strange Mexicans" visited the nearby silver-mining village of Georgetown, attracting the attention of the citizens who conjectured that Pilar and his "notorious gang" were there for the purpose of "murdering or again gaining possession of the girl." The reporter could understand an attempted murder of Reyes Alvarez, her mother, and her brother, since they were the only living witnesses against the lawbreakers. But he could not fathom why the men would try to re-kidnap the maiden, commenting that "there is nothing very attractive in the appearance of the young damsel."

Deputy Sheriff Peter Spencer was sent for, but he was only able to arrest one man, a Silviano Marile, identified by the girl and her family as one of those engaged in her abduction.

Disappointed, Sheriff Spencer blamed his inability to capture the other gang members on the Mexican-American residents of the area, saying, "they either sympathize with or fear them, conceal and give them information on the movements of the officers, making their capture a very difficult undertaking." Sheriff Spencer felt a little better after arresting one Hispanic man "for impeding the officers' search and using insulting language," misdemeanors which cost the fellow a ten dollar fine.

The lawmen and other citizens of the area, however, were determined to capture Pilar Saiz and his accomplices and, as a result, suspicion was aroused that every "Mexican" lawbreaker, or even any stranger, was somehow part of the gang.

In May two mounted officers spotted a Hispanic man running down an arroyo several miles outside of Silver City. Suspecting that he might be Pilar, they gave chase and soon overtook him. They shouted some questions to him which he answered. Then one of the officers attempted to ride up to the man's side. The terrified fellow threw himself down behind a clump of bushes and began to raise his Winchester. The lawman immediately drew his pistol and fired; his bullet passed through the "Mexican's" hat and grazed his scalp. Although momentarily stunned, the cornered man refused to "throw down" his weapon, spunkily suggesting that the officers give up their pistols to him. One deputy then dismounted and threatened to shoot unless the gun was surrendered, but still the man refused. Finally, however, he laid down his weapon and stepped back a few paces so that it could be secured.

Marched off to jail, the prisoner refused to give his real name or any other useful information. No proof that he had been involved in any wrongdoing was forthcoming. Nevertheless, one local newspaper said about the prisoner, "He is evidently a very hard case...that he is a criminal and an outlaw there can be but little doubt." Most of this judgment seems to have been based on the fact that all four of the man's fingers on his left hand had been cut off close to the knuckles, and the first joint of the thumb on the same hand was also missing.[2]

Time passed, and the elusive Pilar remained at large, much to the embarrassment and irritation of area lawmen. In July of that year, Sheriff Peter Spencer arrested a horse thief in the general vicinity of Georgetown. Again, the newspaper reported that the man undoubtedly belonged to "a gang of Mexican thieves and outlaws...it was part of this gang who murdered Deputy Sheriff Hall...they are a hard lot and the sooner they are wiped out entirely the better for the country."

## The *Bandido* and the *Señorita*

Similar sentiments were expressed several times in the newspaper in the months to follow whenever any Spanish-speaking lawbreaker was apprehended for any offense. Pilar and his crime had obviously become the trademark for Hispanic misconduct. Whether or not there was an actual cohesive "gang," as the newspaper editor liked to imply, is questionable.

Ironically, it was Sheriff Spencer who wound up in jail that year, not Pilar. The six-foot-tall constable, known to have a violent temper, was arrested for brutally pistol-whipping a miner, then hauling him off to the *calabozo* and leaving the unconscious man to lie there all night and the following day without medical attention, resulting in the man's death from swelling of the brain.[3]

As 1887 began, the missing Pilar was still absent, but not forgotten. In January, two men were found murdered at their cabin in the general area and, once again, the January 21 issue of the *Silver City Enterprise* conjectured that Pilar might be involved saying, "A Mexican and an American were seen in that vicinity the day before the shooting. There is a belief prevalent that Pilar, who killed Deputy Sheriff Hall last year, was connected with this double crime, as McLean [one of the dead men] is said to have reported the whereabouts of Pilar only last week to the sheriff."

Again, the following month, when two Hispanic outlaws were captured, the newspaper dubbed them "general murderers and horse thieves," and stated, "They are undoubtedly a part of the same gang who murdered Deputy Sheriff Hall and carried the Mexican girl into captivity," concluding with a pious statement that they were all hard cases and surely merited hanging.

As later events were to show, all this was pure rumor and wishful thinking. Pilar was long gone. The only accurate article regarding anyone involved, in any manner, with the case, was published on September 30, 1887, when the newspaper reported that Sheriff Hall's widow was awakened in the middle of the night by the presence of an intruder in her bedroom. The horrified woman began to scream in alarm, the burglar instinctively grabbed her throat and began to choke her and, with strength born of absolute terror, the woman fought her way free. At this point the five Hall children set up a chorus of screams too, routing the interloper. As the intruder fled, Mrs. Hall saw, with amazement, that he was wearing a moccasin on one foot and a boot on the other. The prime suspect was an individual who had been bending his elbow at the local watering holes all night, but the town's lawman was unable to arrest him because several of his cronies testified that he had spent the entire night in a saloon.

Finally, in early December, 1887, the residents of Silver City received the welcome word that Pilar had been discovered in Flagstaff, Arizona, had confessed to his identity, and would be returned to town for trial. Unfortunately, before the month was out they also read, in their newspaper, a notice saying, "The Mexican boy who was shot by Pilar, the murderer of Tom Hall, while the former was attempting to recapture his sister who was being carried off by the bandits, died yesterday morning and was buried by the county in the afternoon."[4]

Rather than having been responsible for just about every crime committed in the Silver City-Georgetown-Pinos Altos-Mimbres River-area for the prior two years, Pilar had fled northward after the Hall shooting. He had gone first to Socorro, then to Albuquerque, and finally headed westward into Arizona, where he laid low by working in a remote sheep camp. Fearful of eventually being found, he had saved one hundred dollars from his meager salary and planned to use it to travel to California.

At some point, the sheriff of Silver City received a tip that Pilar was in the Flagstaff area, so he hired an acquaintance of Pilar's to shadow him. This man finally spotted Pilar one day when he came into Flagstaff from the sheep ranch and pretended to be his friend, but secretly informed the local sheriff. He then talked Pilar into attending a *baile* (dance) with him, and while the unsuspecting fugitive was enjoying himself he was easily captured.[5]

## The *Bandido* and the *Señorita*

Georgetown, a booming silver mining town from 1876 until 1886, fell on hard times, first when hit by a smallpox epidemic, and later when the price of silver dropped drastically. (Library of Congress)

The following June, the outlaw, who now was being called Pilar Perez rather than Pilar Saiz in both newspaper accounts and court documents, was put on trial in Silver City. The proceedings, which took a mere three hours from the time the jury selection was begun until a verdict of murder in the first degree was returned, was obviously nothing more than a mere formality.

Pilar, from the moment of his discovery in Flagstaff the previous fall, consistently contended that Hall had shot at him twice and he had returned fire only in self-defense. This claim he repeated in the courtroom. *Señorita* Alvarez, however, testified differently, reiterating her original story. Pilar, still unwilling to let go of his romantic vision of himself as a Latin lover, accused the girl of telling falsehoods and said, in addition, that he had not abducted her but had "won her away with love." He said they had been eloping until she became frightened when the deputy was shot and killed.

## From Martyrs to Murderers

According to reports, Pilar's court-appointed attorney, an Anglo, "could not say anything in favor of the defendant," so Pilar's proverbial goose was cooked. As the local newspaper put it, "...there was practically no defense, and in a few minutes a verdict was given that sealed his doom."[6]

At the time of his conviction and sentencing, newspaper accounts stated that Pilar showed no particular excitement or emotion. They also reported that in the weeks that followed the jailed prisoner talked about his impending execution dispassionately, and fearlessly joked with other prisoners, saying he would return in spirit to watch them hung. With braggadocio he remarked that since a man was not born to live forever, he might as well die one way as another, and laughingly said he "wanted to go to hell on a black horse."

Less than a month after the trial carpenters were busy erecting a gallows on the north side of the Silver City courthouse.

The basement jail under the Silver City courthouse where Pilar spent his last days on earth. Note electric light, stone floors, and guards. (Silver City, N.M. Museum, John Harlan Collection)

## The *Bandido* and the *Señorita*

With some semblance of decency they were also ordered to erect a high board fence around it, tall enough so people on the hilltops and neighboring houses could not see anyone upon the scaffold. However, sixty officials and people of influence were to be issued tickets admitting them to the area where they could view the proceedings.

On the Monday before his hanging, the death warrant was read to Pilar in Spanish. Later, the local priest came by the jail to talk with the condemned man. Pilar suspended his game of solitaire long enough to confess to the Father and receive the sacrament but did not show any great interest in spiritual or religious matters. In fact, the evening before his hanging, a woman peddler came by his cell and inquired whether he would like to buy any of her fruit or candy. With a straight face Pilar told her, "Well, just to help you out I will buy some items now provided you'll agree to give them to me on credit and come by tomorrow after 4 p.m. for your money."[7]

Whether it was a splendid display of bravado or a real lack of apprehension, Pilar was reported as "the least concerned of any person around the jail," with the possible exception of the man who had been chosen to "pull the rope to let the fatal drop fall." The newspaper stated that the potential hangman "felt honored to be allowed to pull the rope and would not have missed the opportunity to thus distinguish himself for many dollars."

The night before the hanging, Pilar was reported to have slept "as though he had a long life ahead of him," then to have eaten a hearty breakfast and, when asked by the sheriff, at 9:00 a.m., whether he desired anything, replied, "No, I have had plenty."

Less than an hour later the twenty-seven-year-old, described as both good-looking and "by no means stupid," walked out to the gallows. At 9:58 a.m., the sheriff dropped a handkerchief as a signal to the hangman, enclosed in a box out of sight of the spectators. The rope was pulled, Pilar dropped seven feet, and his neck was broken.

In a sad commentary, the newspaper wrote, "There was one thing remarkable about the spectators present; not a single expression of sympathy was manifested for the condemned man during the breathless moments preceding the hanging. It was evident that the murderer had no real friends among the spectators." It is to be wondered whether *Señorita* Reyes Alvarez was present.

Endnotes:

[1] The *Silver City Enterprise*, March 19, 1886. Although the original article stated that the kidnapped girl's brother died five days later from the effects of a serious bullet wound in the leg, the young man, though injured, did not expire.

[2] Ibid., May 28, 1886.

[3] Ibid., August 13, 1886. Constable Spencer, who had earlier been praised by the newspaper when arresting Hispanic citizens, was now castigated for killing a miner named Rodney O'Hara. The editor said that although the constable was known to be hot-headed, he was otherwise favorably regarded by most people. But further reading reveals that much dissatisfaction existed among the residents in regard to what was seen as collusion between the constable and his close friend the town justice of the peace. The victim, O'Hara, was described as something of a slugger, noisy when drunk, and weighing 175 pounds. But Spencer pistol-whipped him unmercifully according to eye-witnesses. The newspaper stated, "The constable certainly had no right to strike O'Hara unless in self-defense, for words do not justify an officer in abusing a prisoner."

[4] Ibid., December 30, 1887.

[5] Ibid., July 6, 1888. An earlier issue of the newspaper (June 8, 1888), reported a different version of Pilar's capture. In that version, Pilar was already in a Flagstaff jail, had revealed his identity and confessed to the shooting, but insisted he shot in self-defense. This was the defense he used during his trial.

[6] Ibid., June 8, 1888.

[7] Ibid., July 6, 1888.

## A Bloody Afternoon in Santa Cruz

A footloose young man can start off on an adventure with nothing more in mind than earning a little money, finding some excitement, seeing new places, and learning what the world is all about. But one thing can lead to another, and eventually he might well find himself involved in appalling situations beyond anything he had ever anticipated. That is what happened to Albert L. Gay.

When Gay headed west on the Santa Fe Trail in the spring of 1847, he really had nothing more in mind than earning a good salary as a civilian teamster employed by the Army Quartermaster. He could send money home to his mother, get a look at the whole new territory out west which had just been "liberated" from Mexico, and possibly find a wonderful spot where he could settle and begin to farm.

Albert Gay, born in the early 1820s in New York State, was adventurous, intelligent, literate, and surprisingly lacking in the narrow-minded prejudices so common among many of the Americans who swept into New Mexico and, in a bloodless invasion, appropriated the area for the United States in 1846.

## From Martyrs to Murderers

Soon after arriving in Santa Fe, Gay was sent to a grazing camp twenty-five miles away to guard government mules and oxen from marauding Indians. During that period, there was a fight between a few of the notoriously rowdy Missouri volunteer soldiers and some of the male Hispanic citizens of the newly-occupied territory. As a result several soldiers were killed. The military then hunted down and shot or took prisoner a number of the local Mexicans. Gay, although an Anglo-American from the East and an Army employee, showed an amazing lack of bias when he described events in a letter home. He wrote:

> I must announce, after having some little opportunity of judging of their character and disposition that the Mexicans are not as bad as our countrymen represent them in the states. In fact there is [sic] two sides to every question, and it is true that some few parties of volunteers have been inhumanly murdered by them, but in every case the volunteers were the aggressors. Volunteers and teamsters are dispersed over various parts of the country herding and not infrequently turn their animals upon the Mexican's corn and wheat and when politely asked to remove them would tell the Mexicans to help themselves if they could. In vain they would tell the volunteers that if their corn and wheat was destroyed they must starve, for that was their only resource.[1]

Gay also told his parents that he frequently visited the local people at their homes, where he was always treated with the utmost kindness, and that he had learned to speak the Spanish language "pretty well."

After three months, however, the quiet life at the grazing camp began to pall and when Albert Gay heard that a volunteer company of dragoons was being raised in Santa Fe. He managed to join, becoming a private in Captain Grove's Company B, Santa Fe Rifles.[2]

The Mexican-American War was still in progress on August 6, 1847, when Gay wrote home saying he would probably be

# A Bloody Afternoon

> "Santa Fee August 26th 1847
>
> Dear Parents
>         A notion having entered my
> (concluded) mind to send you a few lines, by way
> of giving you what information I have at hand
> and removing from your minds, any uneasiness
> that my sojourn here may have occasioned.
> There is nothing in the line of news, of any
> stirring importance here at present; Some seven
> Companies of new Volunteers have arrived within
> the last few days; and others are on the way
> to the am't of 18 companies, and who will be
> here in a few days, thus making the force in
> New Mexico 3000 strong — what disposition will be
> made of these here I do not know but presume
> some will go to Oregon, others to Chihuha, and
> probably the Santa Fe Battallion, to which I
> belong will go there. This Command consists of
> 4 companies under Major Walker, one of Infantry,
> and 3 of mounted men. to the latter I belong — am
> in Capt Groves Co — B. Prices Rangers — for a
> compensation we receive $8 per month. per man
> and $12 for horse: probably $6 for forage. $1 per
> month for use of my Rifle (all not having R) making
> $27 per Month. The Labor which we have to do
> is nominal, Drill at 8 o° AM & 5 ᵉ PM, and
> roll call at sunrise, and stand guard once in
> ten days — for my part I find it very agreeable
> for I attend a Spanish School every day, and am

Copy of one of Albert L. Gay's letters.
(Gay Family and Sandoval County Historical Archives)

sent to Chihuahua, Mexico, which Colonel Alexander Doniphan had captured five months earlier. Gay would indeed see Chihuahua, but not for seven months, and not until he had seen Indian country first.

His distraught mother, seeing, as the young private apparently did not, that with his enlistment he had set his life on a different and more dangerous path, wrote to a family member, "I fear before he is again at liberty he will find something harder to do than he ever did before. I hope he may live to return but it is very doubtful." Prophetic words, at least in part, for Albert Gay would eventually be forced to do something which ran counter to his kind and accepting nature.

For a short time Private Gay found military life "very agreeable." He was earning twenty-seven dollars a month and had little to do other than drill morning and evening and stand guard once every ten days. Albert Gay spent his resulting free time in a very different way, which set him apart from most of the other soldiers. Instead of carousing, he attended the only school in New Mexico. It was taught in Spanish, and the enrollment consisted of twenty boys, all excellent scholars from the more affluent first families of Santa Fe. In an August 26, 1847, letter to his parents, Gay described Santa Fe, saying, "Of all places, this is the beat for gambling and licentiousness, drinking not being excepted. In fact every house in town is a whore house or a grog shop."

This idyllic military life was short-lived, however, and by September 1, 1847, the battalion left the city on an expedition against the troublesome Navajos. After following the Rio Grande southward for seventy-five miles, the units turned west, marching about one hundred miles to a point where they were forced to leave their supply wagons. From there they pushed on to Zuñi Pueblo and, after a short stop, continued on another one hundred miles to *Cañón de Chelly*, the Navajo stronghold in northeastern Arizona.

After this laborious march the exhausted troops were virtually out of provisions. Even worse, in an area they believed held "5000 fighting men," they couldn't find even a single Navajo

# A Bloody Afternoon

(*above*) Zuñi Pueblo, in western New Mexico, as it appeared in 1879, virtually unchanged from when the inhabitants fed the hungry soldiers. (Smithsonian Institution) (*below*) The almost perpendicular walls of Cañón de Chelly in northeastern Arizona. (Author's Collection)

brave. Finally, completely out of food, they marched to the mouth of the canyon, hoping to find sheep or other Indian livestock to eat. Instead they found only a small group of Navajos, who managed to outwit them and escape.

After several days without food, Gay's unit found an Indian mule and several dogs, which they devoured. The following day a lieutenant and twenty-four men, including Gay, were ordered to return the 125 miles to Zuñi to obtain provisions to be sent back to the starving troops. By the time they reached the pueblo the men were so weak they could barely stand, and the next day Gay's horse died from exhaustion. The friendly Zuñis treated them kindly and also dispatched food to their half-famished companions.

In a letter home Albert Gay described the Zuñis as "highly intelligent, more so than the civilized Indians in the states, and withal very industrious, raising plenty of corn and wheat, and making such domestick [sic] articles as they need."[3]

After the unsuccessful Indian campaign the troops made their way back to the Rio Grande, where they set up camp and remained awaiting a provisions train from Santa Fe. It was now November, and they learned that Mexico City had fallen to the American Army in September. Private Gay and his companions expected that the war would soon be ended and peace declared. They figured they would never see Mexico. They were very wrong.

Throughout the winter General Sterling Price, the military governor of New Mexico, kept some troops at Socorro and others at Albuquerque, southern points from which he could quickly dispatch them to Mexico if he received word from Washington to do so. The War Department, however, had told Price he could attack only if he learned of an enemy force being organized in Chihuahua "with the design of marching on New Mexico."[4]

However, in Santa Fe, American merchants and the newspapers kept putting pressure on Price to mount an expedition against the Mexicans. Their interest was purely mercenary, for Chihuahua was an important trading center for them, but their desires happened to parallel Price's own personal inclination.

## A Bloody Afternoon

The justification presented itself in early February, 1848. Rumors began flying northward from the El Paso area that a Mexican general was advancing on that city with an army of thousands. When the word reached Socorro, where Gay's unit and others were wintering, the companies immediately took up the line of march for El Paso, without waiting for orders from Santa Fe.

At 8:00 p.m., on February 3, 1848, the troopers were told they would be leaving at dawn to march southward, in an attempt to save the five hundred American soldiers at El Paso. Two hours later, after packing his gear, Albert Gay managed to pen a brief letter home. By flickering candlelight he wrote that "about the 8th of Feb. you will probably hear that we are all whipped and killed or that after hard fighting we have come off victorious. I know not what our fate may be but I expect no evil, and if I am to be killed in Battle it is a consolation to know that I have not to die but once...but I have no notion of dying."

But, after rushing southward, Albert Gay and the other soldiers found El Paso peaceful when they arrived. The rumor had been nothing more than that—a rumor. Sadly enough, however, the rumor, along with the slow communications of that period, set off a chain of events which would result in an orgy of needless suffering and death.

Two days before General Price's Santa Fe office even received word of the purported enemy march on El Paso, a peace treaty had been signed between the United States and Mexico at Guadalupe Hildago, a suburb of Mexico City. The war was finished! Within days the governors of the Mexican states were notified that all fighting was to cease.

Price, of course, knew nothing of this. When he arrived in El Paso in late February 1848, bringing additional troops from Santa Fe with him, he learned, as Gay and the others had, that no Mexican force was advancing on the city. While he was encamped there he also received a dispatch from Washington which, although written the previous November, nevertheless forbade him to proceed south. Deliberately, Price decided to ignore, and thus disobey, the orders—an action which would have terrible consequences.

# From Martyrs to Murderers

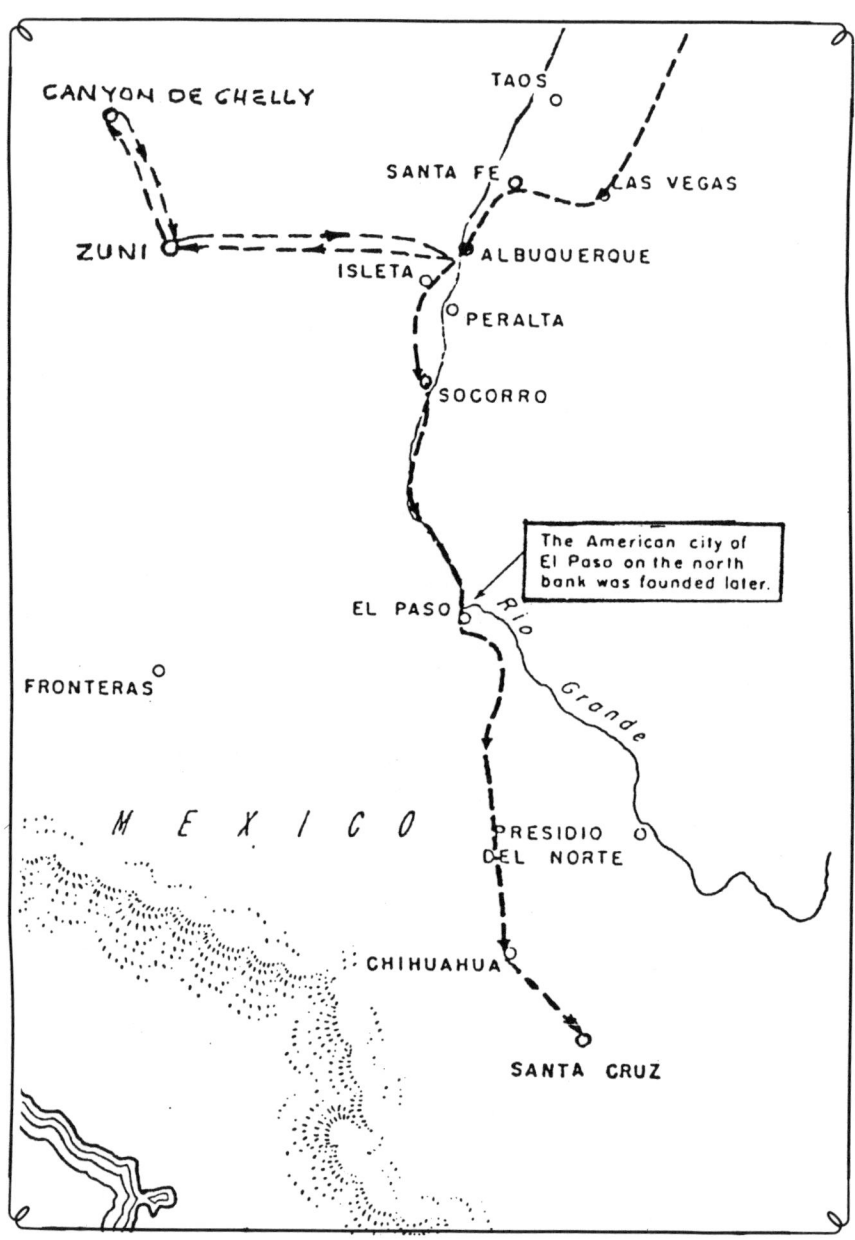

Route taken by Private Gay's company from September 1, 1847, when they left Santa Fe, until March 16, 1848, when they fought the battle at Santa Cruz. (Map drawn by Charles Meketa)

# A Bloody Afternoon

General Sterling Price
(*Harper's Pictorial of the History of the Civil War*, 1866)

Although he had to wait in El Paso for his slower-moving supply trains to arrive from the north, Price, determined to have his fight, began military operations immediately. He quickly dispatched some of his best mounted troops to Carrizal, ninety miles to the south, to cut off the Mexican's communications to and from Chihuahua City. He chose the three volunteer companies under Major Robert Walker's command. This included, of course, Private A. L. Gay, who, in nine short months found his situation changed from that of a peaceful civilian teamster to a mounted soldier, driving over a boundary and deep into a foreign country.

On March 4, the impatient General Price, still without the awaited supplies, crossed into Mexico and joined Walker's unit. The next two days the combined force pressed an additional ninety miles southward in a fatiguing forced march. When they neared Chihuahua, Price's men were met by a delegation from the governor, Angel Trias, who informed them that a peace treaty was in effect and all hostilities suspended.

Price, now committed to the operation he had so recklessly begun, and fearing that Trias' information might be only a strategy to gain time to further fortify the city, rejected the intelligence out-of-hand. He rushed his command forward rapidly but found, when he arrived at Chihuahua, that Trias had evacuated the city and moved southward to avoid any confrontation.

Not content with having captured the city, Price was determined to do battle. There were only enough fresh horses available to mount 250 men. Taking this small contingent, Price pushed ahead and, by March 9, after a hard sixty-mile ride, arrived at Santa Cruz de Rosales where Trias' troops were entrenched in the fortified town.[5]

While awaiting the balance of his force, including his artillery and supply wagons, Price laid close siege on Santa Cruz, but allowed non-combatants to leave if they wished.

Ironically, on March 10, 1848, while Price waited to pounce on the besieged town, the United States Senate, after intense debate, ratified the Treaty of Guadalupe Hildago. The Mexican-American War was officially over!

When Albert Gay watched the first red streaks of sunrise break over the horizon on March 16, he may have seen the scarlet rays as a portent of the bloody day ahead. He knew that Price's command had now been reinforced by the arrival of three companies of Regulars and a battery of cannon.

General Price now demanded the surrender of the town and Governor Trias again informed him that he had received official word that a peace treaty had been concluded, and therefore, they should not do battle. Price, having personally received no confirmation of this news from any official sources, repudiated Trias's claim. Trias, as a matter of honor, then refused to surrender the town saying his troops would defend it if required.

At 10:30 a.m. the American battery opened fire on Santa Cruz.[6] The Mexicans returned in kind and the cannonade went

## A Bloody Afternoon

on for the best part of the day. Later, one American participant ruefully stated, "Our artillery laid to dust the work of years as it played upon their splendid churches and well-constructed houses."

In the late afternoon Price decided it would be necessary to take the town by storm. He ceased his artillery fire, dismounted Gay's company and the rest of his volunteers, and placed them on the west, south, and northwest sides of Santa Cruz. He kept his Regular Army dragoons mounted to cut off any enemy escape attempt or to meet any reinforcements that might appear.

The roar of a cannon burst signaled time for the attack to commence and the volunteers rushed the town amid loud shrieks and cheers. As part of Walker's Santa Fe Battalion, Gay charged from the south. In short order it became obvious to the Americans that fierce house-to-house fighting would be required.

Every structure was filled with brave Mexicans determined to defend their homes. Mexican sharpshooters were posted on the roofs behind parapets and hastily constructed barricades. The volunteers, quickly adapting to this new kind of fighting, advanced on the rooftops and through the streets, breaking into houses with axes and crowbars, killing or driving their enemies out, and then using the homes for cover as they advanced. The Mexicans threw long-fused grenades at the Americans, but the Americans had time to kick them back into enemy-held buildings where they exploded, killing the Mexican soldiers.

Major Walker handed shells from his small mountain howitzer to his men. They were able to light them and use them as hand grenades.

Through the chaos of smoke, gunfire, screams of the wounded, and bursts of artillery fire, Gay and his comrades fought their way, foot by bloody foot, to the large church on the plaza in the center of town where the main Mexican resistance was concentrated. Walker's force battled so vigorously they were cited for having been "in the lead, entering the square fifteen minutes ahead of the other troops." It was sundown when they reached it and prepared to storm the church. However, when Major Walker's howitzer opened fire on the building, the Mexicans raised the white flag.

It was reported that many Mexicans were brutally slain while attempting to surrender. The Missouri Volunteers, still in a frenzy of fighting and killing, were so intent on taking the church the American officers had a difficult time restraining them when the Mexicans gave up.

Darkness soon covered the carnage but the following morning a horrible picture revealed itself. Inflamed passions from the height of battle had had time to cool and the Americans saw bloodied and broken Mexican bodies everywhere—in the streets, on the rooftops, in the homes. More than 250 Mexicans had died defending the town. Amazingly, the Americans lost only four killed and nineteen wounded.

As a result of this unnecessary battle, fought after peace had been signed, and for no apparent motive other than his own political advantage or personal glory, Price was acclaimed a great hero. President Polk considered the campaign one of the notable successes of the war and Missouri newspapers were filled with praise.[7] No one seemed to question the morality of slaughtering hundreds of Mexican soldiers and civilians in needless combat.

But one is left to wonder how Private Albert Gay and many of his fellow volunteers felt later, upon learning that the battle had been without military merit. They had risked their lives through many fearful hours, killed to avoid being killed, and stared, in the cold light of the next dawn, at the ashen faces and torn bodies of those they had slaughtered.

Unfortunately, even though a number of Private Gay's letters were preserved over the years, the one he wrote from Chihuahua in the Spring of 1848 is missing. It was in this correspondence, which he cited in a later letter, that he most probably described the battle, its aftermath, and the emotions he experienced regarding them. It is frustrating that this most vital missive is the one which has failed to survive.

# A Bloody Afternoon

After the battle, Albert Gay and his companions remained in Mexico until early July, acting as part of an army of occupation. He then began a return trip up the Rio Grande to Santa Fe and then eastward on the Santa Fe Trail. He arrived in Independence, Missouri, on October 7, 1848, after "a constant and severe journey of three months from Chihuahua," and was discharged from the military.[8]

At that time he expressed a feeling of great anxiety and insecurity, saying, "Now that I am once more free to think and act and do for myself, I am completely lost...I know not where to go, nor wither to direct my steps—there is a void in my brain, an aching in my heart, that is difficult to be accounted for by those who have not been similarly situated."

Although he had contemplated it, Albert Gay never returned to his Rochester, New York, home to see his parents. Instead, the following Spring, he became a forty-niner, traveling from Missouri to Sacramento via the California Trail. He made a life there, married, established a farm, and dabbled in other enterprises. He died in California in 1867 while only in his early forties.[9]

Without a doubt he never forgot the most eventful afternoon of his life, when he and his comrades faced death in the dusty streets of Santa Cruz de Rosales fighting a battle which never should have occurred.

## Endnotes:

[1] A. L. Gay to parents, Santa Fe, August 6, 1847, Martha Liebert Library Archives, Bernalillo, New Mexico. Photocopies of all Gay's letters cited here, as well as some he and his wife wrote later from California, are on file at the library.

[2] Private A. L. Gay Military Service Records, National Archives, Washington, D.C. Although the Muster-in-Rolls listed the unit as the New Mexican Mounted Volunteers, it was quickly designated as Walker's Santa Fe Battalion, Missouri Mounted Volunteers. The Battalion consisted of three companies of horsemen and one of artillery, commanded by Major

Robert Walker. Gay's horse was valued at thirty dollars and his saddle and equipment at eight dollars.

[3] A. L. Gay to parents, Rio Grande, 150 m's s of Santa Fe, New Mexico, November 10, 1847.

[4] Robert E. Shalhope, Sterling Price, Portrait of a Southerner (Columbia: .lh 7.5
University of Missouri Press, 1971), pp. 70-71.

[5] M. H. Thomlinson, "The Dragoons and El Paso, 1848, New Mexico Historical Review 23, No. 3 (July 1948): 218-21; George W. Smith and Charles Judah, eds., Chronicles of the Gringos (Albuquerque: University of New Mexico Press, 1968), p. 143.

[6] Santa Fe Republican, April 22, 1848. Other quoted descriptions of the battle are from this source.

[7] Shalhope, p. 75.

[8] A. L. Gay to parents, Independence, Missouri, October 22, 1848.

[9] Captain Jesse B. Gay, Jr., USN (Ret.), Falls Church, Virginia, to author, July 22, 1986. Captain Gay stated that family records do not show Albert Gay's birth date but list his next-older brother as being born in 1818 in Fort Edward, New York.

# A Singular Friendship

To the Catholic nuns and priests in the small caravan of wagons pushing ever westward across the vast plains under the August sun in 1852, the trip seemed interminable. They had been on the Santa Fe Trail for more than a month and, in that time, many of their party became ill and some had died. Wild storms filled with thunder, lightning, and great downpours had buffeted them as they struggled across the treeless prairie.

The great solitude and vast distances were frightening to those never before exposed to the open wilderness. Frequently their wagons broke down, causing inconvenience and delays. On one occasion their small caravan was followed and watched for a whole day by more than three hundred Indians. Fortunately for the frightened travelers they were not attacked, but thereafter the bishop in charge decreed that they would rest during the day and travel at night saying, "Indians do not usually attack after dark."[1]

Then, one morning, just as they were about to set up camp, they spotted a halted train of twenty-five wagons. As they drew closer the clerics observed Mexican teamsters carrying a man into an isolated and abandoned sod hut.

When the bishop, Jean Baptiste Lamy, inquired about the proceedings, the Mexicans said they were sure the man had cholera, and they refused to travel any further with him for fear of contracting the deadly disease. They also gave a name to the man they were deserting—Levi Spiegelberg.

The bishop entered the tumble-down hut. Even though, only a few weeks earlier Lamy's party of clerics had fallen victim to the same disease, and the Mother Superior of the traveling nuns had died of it, Lamy told the suffering man, "Good friend, we willingly make room for you in our covered wagon, and we will nurse you until you regain your strength, for we could not think of leaving you here in this lonely prairie cabin...we are not afraid of contagion."[2]

Thus began a most unusual and splendid friendship between two men who, at first glance, seemed worlds apart, yet had much more in common than most. The harmonious relationship not only had a strong impact on Santa Fe's history but, also generated some interesting tales.

Lamy, the French-born prelate, was sent to New Mexico in 1851 after it became part of the United States. His mission was to institute progressive programs among the Catholic Hispaños who comprised most of the population. When he arrived, the Territory was primitive and impoverished, the people poor and illiterate, and Indian raids still commonplace. There were few priests, and the humble adobe churches had dirt floors, no pews, and leaking roofs. It took almost superhuman efforts on his part over the next few decades not only to provide the populace with proper religious observances but also to supply them with needed social services, ranging from education to medical care.

Levi Spiegelberg was a Prussian-born Jew whose eldest brother, Solomon Jacob, had arrived in New Mexico in 1846 at the age of twenty, and soon become a sutler supplying the United States Army. Before long, S. J., as he was known, launched a general merchandise firm in Santa Fe and sent to Europe for Levi to come help. As the business expanded throughout the Territory, three other brothers arrived, one at a time, to join the venture.[3] Eventually the family became very

# A Singular Friendship

prominent civic leaders in Santa Fe and their interests in retail and wholesale merchandising evolved into even more widespread investments.

By the time the wagon train reached Santa Fe, young Levi was almost well and the incident developed strong ties between the Catholic bishop and the grateful Spiegelbergs. During the next few years, as the bishop struggled to build the necessary cohesive religious organization to serve his flock in that poverty-stricken area and the Spiegelbergs worked to create a wide network of merchandise establishments, suppliers, and customers, they often helped each other. Thus, the hardships they all faced, their mutual European cultural background, and their great isolation in the pioneer Southwest of the mid-1800s helped forge this unique friendship.

There were few Jews in predominately Catholic Santa Fe in those early days and no synagogue. As a result, Yom Kippur and other religious ceremonies were held in private homes. Bishop Lamy was usually present and always brought wine, fruit, and flowers from his garden as gifts. When, in turn, the bishop was trying to raise money to build a cathedral, the Spiegelberg family donated five hundred dollars, a considerable sum for those days.[4]

Above the main archway of the cathedral is a keystone which has long been an item of discussion, research, and controversy. It contains a triangle, within which is inscribed, in bold Hebrew characters, the word Adonai. Upon seeing it, Flora Spiegelberg is reputed to have cried in surprise, "Monseigneur, you have not only preached the Fatherhood of God and the Brotherhood of Man, irrespective of race, creed, or color, but you have practiced it daily."[5] What Lamy replied has not been recorded for posterity.

But for many decades the common perception was that this keystone was Lamy's way of symbolizing his friendship and gratitude to the Jewish community of Santa Fe. However, in recent years a number of scholars have demonstrated that the Hebrew inscription within a triangle was a commonly used design symbolizing the Christian doctrine of the Holy Trinity.

(*above*) The Spiegelberg Brothers. *l. to r.*: Willi, whose wife was a special friend to the Archbishop, Emanuel, S. J. (or Jacob) who established the successful family businesses, Levi, whose life was saved by the Archbishop, and Lehman. (*below*) One of several stores the successful Spiegelberg brothers established in various New Mexico towns. (Museum of New Mexico)

## A Singular Friendship

Nevertheless, for Flora Spiegelberg, the keystone always represented both a personal friendship and the harmony which existed between Jews and Catholics in early Santa Fe.

Eventually, Levi Spiegelberg moved to New York to serve as a purchasing agent for the New Mexico enterprise, two of the brothers left the business, and a fourth was tragically crushed to death in the collapse of a weakened adobe wall. From then on only two brothers, Lehman and Willi, were the "Santa Fe" Spiegelbergs. But they and their families remained close friends of the bishop. Willi sometimes recounted the story of how he, like Levi, almost lost his life while crossing the Santa Fe Trail, describing how he barely escaped being massacred by the Kaw Indians in 1861.

Bishop Lamy loved to garden, and brought into Santa Fe many seeds, plants, nuts, and bulbs, from the East and from Europe. He shared these items, not available locally, with Flora Spiegelberg, Willi's wife, who was especially close to him. An educated and cultured woman, she was able to converse with Lamy in his native French, and the two often traded gardening tips and surplus fruits and vegetables from their plots.

One morning, after moving into her newly-constructed home, Flora looked out to see this eminent Catholic clergyman on his knees, planting a pair of willow saplings by her gate, and then placing a blessing on them, the home, and its inhabitants. Several years later, in a return gesture, Flora presented Lamy with an olive-wood rosary she had had blessed in Jerusalem and at the Vatican.

Probably the most revered sacred object for Santa Fe Catholics is a tiny statue of the Madonna, made of painted gesso and wood and called *La Conquistadora*. Steeped in history, it was brought to New Mexico by the first European settlers, Juan de Oñate's party, in 1598. It was taken to Mexico when the Spanish settlers were driven out by the Indians during the Pueblo Rebellion of 1680, and then returned once again during the reconquest in 1692.

Every May the statue, dressed in beautiful robes and carried on an ornate, canopied litter, is taken from its usual location in

Santa Fe's St. Francis Cathedral, Lamy's pride and joy. His friends, the Spiegelbergs, contributed generously to construction costs. The tall towers in the drawing were never actually completed. *(upper l.)* Archbishop Lamy. (Ritch, 1885) *(upper r.)* This statue was known as "La Conquistadora" because it accompanied the Spanish soldiers when they successfully recaptured Santa Fe in 1693 after being driven from New Mexico by the 1680 Pueblo Indian Revolt. The statue was taken as a plaything by a Spiegelberg child. (Robert H. Martin photo, Museum of New Mexico)

## A Singular Friendship

a Santa Fe chapel and transported by the faithful through the streets in a religious procession.

One year during the ceremonial march, the men carrying *La Conquistadora* stopped to pray at a spot near the home of Willi Spiegelberg and put the litter down. Unnoticed by anyone, the littlest Spiegelberg, a girl of only four or five, slipped through the crowd and plucked the beautiful "doll" from its canopied recess. The loss was not discovered until later at the cathedral, and the mystery of the disappearance caused astonishment, concern, and even fear among the participants. Some of the more superstitious felt the departure had been of a supernatural origin.

That evening, when Flora Spiegelberg kissed her daughter good night, she found the statue on the bed pillow where the child had placed it. Horrified that this most revered object had been treated as a plaything, Mrs. Spiegelberg rushed to the bishop's house to return it with profuse and embarrassed apologies.

Bishop Lamy listened to her explanation, then "roared with laughter," and comforted his apprehensive friend with a glass of wine and assurances. Many months later a beautifully dressed wax doll from Paris arrived at the Spiegelberg home with a note to the little girl, telling her it was "to replace the little Madonna" which had been taken away from her.[6]

As New Mexico's economy expanded over the years, so did the Spiegelberg brothers' influence and success. They spread their commercial interests into mining, real estate, insurance and construction. They also served as sutlers and mail route contractors for several Army posts and Indian agencies and finally, to protect their own interests, established a bank in Santa Fe in 1872.

Bishop Lamy, during this time, had built a diocesan see that contained numerous churches and well-trained clergy, schools, hospitals, convents, and even orphanages. While the Spiegelbergs dominated the social life of Santa Fe, Bishop Lamy dominated the spiritual. Both were extremely powerful.

In 1875 Lamy was elevated to archbishop of New Mexico. Prominent in planning the celebration for the ordination of this

Catholic prelate was Flora Spiegelberg, the Jewish grande dame of Santa Fe. And it was her husband, Willi, who presided over the formal dinner following the ceremonies, attended by papal delegates from Rome and the archbishops of Arizona and Colorado.

When President and Mrs. Rutherford B. Hayes visited the city in 1880, accompanied by General William Tecumseh Sherman, it was at the home of Lehman Spiegelberg that they dined, and among the guests, of course, was Archbishop Lamy.

On February 13, 1888, church bells all over Santa Fe began a mournful toll. Lehman and Willi Spiegelberg knew what that meant. Their long-time friend, Archbishop Lamy, frail and elderly, had died. This marked the passing of an era. Within five years, by 1893, the last of the Spiegelberg family's interests in New Mexico were liquidated and the brothers returned to the East. They had, however, left an indelible mark on New Mexico, as had Jean Baptiste Lamy.

Because of the Spiegelberg family's pioneering work, a large Jewish presence in the Southwest was established, and great progress made in modernizing the area. Because of Lamy's selfless dedication to early New Mexico's Catholics, opportunities for education, health care, and spiritual support were made available to them. And that splendid friendship between people of such disparate religious beliefs served as a beautiful example of conduct in the tri-cultural mixing pot of colorful early New Mexico.

Endnotes:

[1] Paul Horgan, *Lamy of Santa Fe* (New York: Farrar, Straus and Giroux, 1975), p. 163.

[2] Ibid., p. 164.

[3] Michael L. Lawson, "Flora Langermann Spiegelberg: Grand Lady of Santa Fe," *Western States Jewish Historical Quarterly* 8 (July 1976): pp. 194-95.

[4] Horgan, p. 359.

[5] Lawson, p. 299.

[6] Horgan, pp. 415-16.

# Let Me Die With Honor

Some men bring misfortune upon themselves by courting disaster. Others are innocent victims of a malevolent Fate. With John G. Atkinson, it seemed to be a combination of these two factors. Certainly his audacious personality pushed him into a lifestyle filled with potentially dangerous situations, but it must also be said that Lady Luck sometimes abandoned him.

Born in Sunderland, England, in 1838, young Atkinson emigrated to America and lived in North Carolina for a time. Later, lured by the prospect of a quick and easy fortune, he, like many others, undertook the long and hazardous trip to California's gold fields.[1]

The wished-for fortune, however, did not materialize, and by the summer of 1861, Atkinson was ready for a new adventure. California had issued a call for volunteers to enlist in an army being raised to march eastward to New Mexico to aid the inhabitants of that Territory which had been invaded by a Confederate Army of Texans. The twenty-three-year-old Atkinson quickly enlisted, becoming part of Colonel James H. Carleton's California Column.

# From Martyrs to Murderers

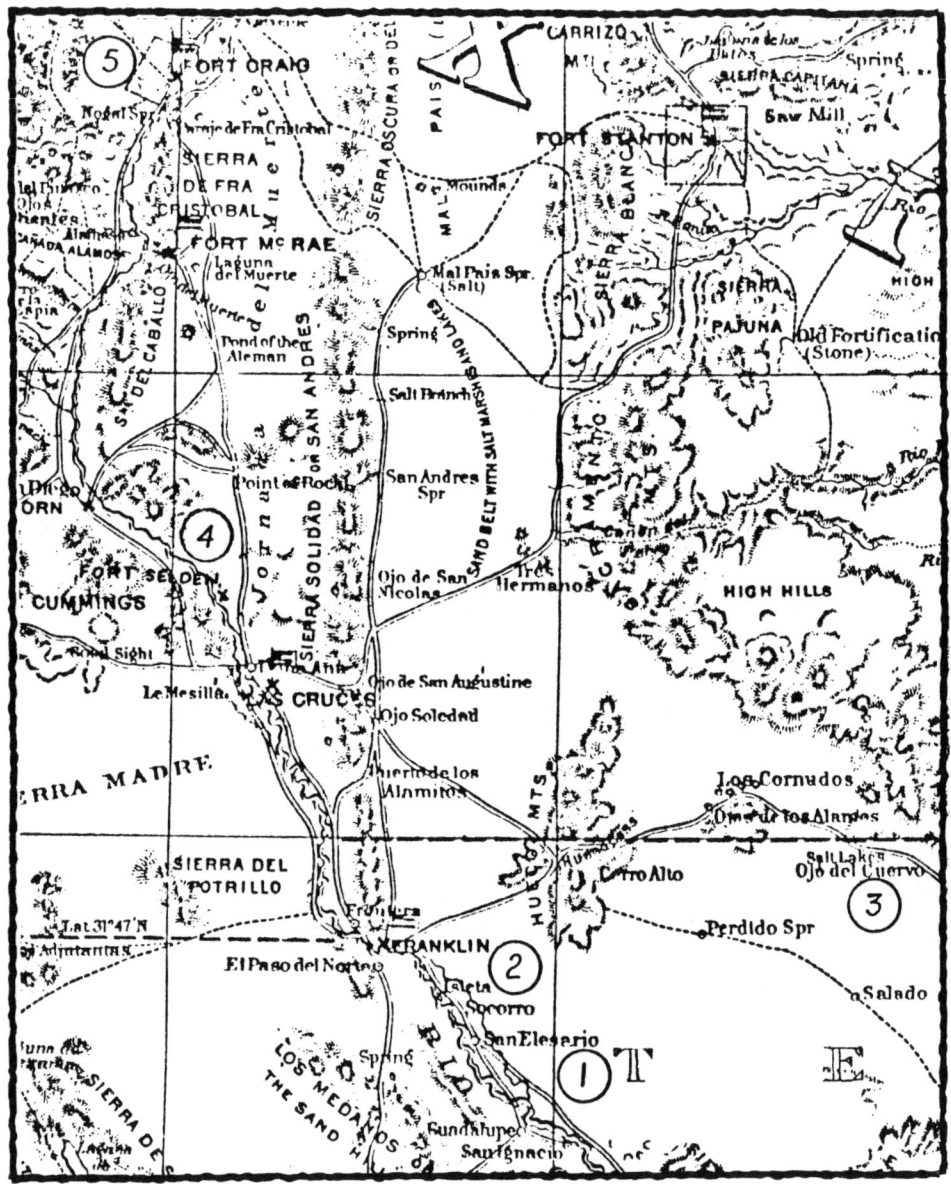

Enlarged portion of an 1864 Army map showing the area of the Salt War. (#1) San Elizario, Texas, separated from the Mexican state of Chihuahua only by the Rio Grande. (#2) Franklin, Texas, now known as El Paso. (#3) Area of the disputed salt lakes. (#4) Fort Selden, New Mexico, where Atkinson was stationed when shot in the drunken brawl. (#5) Fort Craig, New Mexico, Atkinson's first duty station as a New Mexico volunteer soldier. (Author's Collection)

## Let Me Die

After an eight-hundred-mile trek across deserts and through Indian country, the Californians arrived at the Rio Grande in March, 1862, only to find that the Rebels had already been defeated and driven out. For the balance of their enlistments, the California Volunteers served as Indian fighters and did garrison duty in New Mexico.

Before Atkinson's tour was completed, however, he arranged to be mustered out of his company in order to immediately re-enlist in a newly-established regiment of New Mexico infantry volunteers. This action, which was common, allowed him to jump in rank from private to sergeant almost overnight.[2] Atkinson's new company was stationed at the second largest fort in New Mexico, Fort Craig, situated on the banks of the Rio Grande half way between El Paso and Santa Fe.

Although Fort Craig was considered an excellent duty station by most of the soldiers, one man assigned there wrote home complaining of "the same monotonous routine from morning till night," and a very limited diet composed almost exclusively of "bread, bacon, greens, coffee, and water to drink."[3]

That writer also described the local women as "ugly as sin," but apparently Atkinson did not find them so. His service record shows that shortly after he joined the company Atkinson began treatment for gonorrhea, followed closely by a six-week intermittent course of treatments for syphilis. For the next two years Atkinson reported to sick call for a variety of ailments, ranging from an ulcerated thumb to diarrhea, and from tonsillitis to unspecified fevers. He also underwent several more syphilis treatments.[4] Whether he was a malingerer or actually in bad health, Atkinson did spend a lot of time off duty, but was still able to retain his rank as sergeant for most of the period.

One reason for this was his heroism during a river-crossing accident which took six lives — two military officers, a civilian, and three enlisted men — from Atkinson's company. In May 1865, Atkinson's company was sent to southern New Mexico to begin construction of a new post, Fort Selden. As they left Fort Craig, the command attempted to cross a Rio Grande made violent and dangerous by the spring runoff of melted snow from the northern mountains. One successful crossing was made on a rather primitive ferry, but, when a second was tried, the ferry was caught by the force of the midstream current and water flooded over the bow. A number of men and animals were swept overboard and the out-of-control boat was buffeted by the current until, in panic, most of those remaining aboard either jumped into the river or lost their grip and were swept away. Atkinson and a lieutenant were singled out and cited for "using every exertion from the shore for the benefit of the drowning men, and were the means of saving several lives."[5]

For the next eighteen months Company F, Atkinson's unit, was employed in the construction of Fort Selden on the cottonwood-lined banks of the Rio Grande in southern New Mexico. The primitive post of one-story adobe buildings, with flat, dirt-covered roofs and earthen floors, not only lacked most amenities but also offered little in the way of entertainment. So, Sergeant Atkinson, a man who liked a good time, was probably very pleased to be put on detached service to travel to Fort Bliss, Texas, in the summer of 1866.

Within three days his business was done at the fort and Atkinson left Bliss to rejoin his company. He could not resist, however, stopping in El Paso. There, in his own words, he "was shot by two noncommissioned officers of the U. S. Army who, being crazy drunk, mistook me for one Major Jackson with whom they had a difficulty."[6] Atkinson, shot in the right hip during the drunken brawl, was treated by the post surgeons at Fort Bliss. He was hospitalized for seven months and the shattered hip joint healed in such a way that he was crippled for life. Thereafter he was known as 'Limpin' John.'

One of his attackers, a Sergeant Wheater of the 5th U. S. Infantry, was found guilty by the civil authorities, and sentenced to two years in the Texas penitentiary, but managed to escape from the sheriff's custody and fled. Wheater, however, did meet with a sort of poetic justice. Two years later, irate at some other person with whom he was having problems, Wheater set fire to the man's tent. He received two bullets for his trouble—one

## Let Me Die

through the body and the second through his head—thus ending his career as a troublemaker.[7]

When his hip was sufficiently healed, Atkinson was discharged from the hospital in January 1867, and returned to civilian life. He decided to remain in El Paso County. Within a few years he had made a number of influential friends, and an equal number of vehement enemies. The area, like many others in the early West, contained two factions which were constantly vying for power and money. Unfortunately for 'Limpin' John,' one of his most bitter enemies was a politician, customs collector, and general entrepreneur named W. W. Mills, who lived to be an old man and wrote a book about El Paso's early days. As a result, Mills' obviously biased opinions of Atkinson's character and actions make up most of the surviving information about the balance of Atkinson's life.

One of Atkinson's friends was Sheriff Charles Ellis, who had been a fellow California volunteer soldier. For a time, in the early 1870s, Atkinson served as one of his deputies in El Paso County. It has been alleged, perhaps unfairly, that Atkinson's overbearing nature and use of the power of his position made him unpopular among the Hispanic inhabitants of San Elizario, the nearby county seat. Mills asserted that, for no valid reason, Atkinson arrested him and his brother one day when they rode into town. They were charged with violating a state law against carrying arms "except when traveling." The local justice of the peace released the Mills brothers, but Mills further accused Atkinson of approaching him at a party that night and insulting him.[8]

Whatever the truth of the story, Atkinson continued to live in the area, dabbling in politics, opening a mercantile business and, reputedly, enjoying himself in other ways. Although Atkinson had a slight difference in the length of his legs as a result of being shot, it apparently was not a serious impediment when the necessity for some fast running arose after a Mr. Campbell "caught him being agreeable to his wife and took out after him with a pistol."[9] Atkinson, then in his early thirties, was described as five feet eight inches tall, with gray eyes, brown hair, a fair complexion, and lean build. Strong-willed, even dictatorial, and quite brash, he cut a rather swashbuckling figure around town.

Even though John Atkinson was well pleased with the growing wealth he was accumulating and the stature he had acquired in this little town of San Elizario just a few miles southeast of El Paso, events were taking place which would soon cut short his life.

About one hundred miles northeast of El Paso lie salt lakes, which, for centuries, had been the source of salt for Indians and Mexicans on both sides of the border—some coming from as far away as Chihuahua for their supply. The lakes had always been viewed as communal public property and the salt free for the taking. But, in 1877, Charles Howard, seeing what he thought was an overlooked golden opportunity, obtained private claims for the lakes and planned to sell the salt. Howard, a former Confederate soldier from Austin, was a politician, judge, and Atkinson's friend.

A Mexican cart similar to those used to haul salt from the salt lakes in the early days. (Harpers)

When the Mexicans from across the river, as well as the Mexican-Americans in the area, learned of Howard's actions, they were incensed. They hurried to see Luis Cardis, a former legislator and man of influence who was sympathetic to the Mexican populace. Cardis and Howard had been friends before a disagreement ended their camaraderie.

Even though Cardis agreed with the Hispanics' cause, he suggested they return to their homes peacefully and fight the matter in court. The outraged Mexicans, however, formed a mob and confronted Howard. In order to save his life, Howard was forced to sign over his claims to the salt lakes and promise to leave the area and never return. He was compelled to post a bond of twelve thousand dollars to back his promise. Atkinson and Sheriff Ellis, who was also a local merchant, stood as his guarantors.

That might have been the end of the matter if Howard had not been so arrogant and headstrong. Instead of keeping his promise, he merely retired just over the border in Mesilla, New Mexico, and fired off telegrams to the Governor of Texas complaining about the "lawless" Mexicans, and demanding troops. He chose to ignore the fact that Cardis, a peaceful man, had actually kept the Hispaños from assassinating him. Instead, he charged Cardis with being the chief conspirator.

On October 9, 1877, when a detachment of U. S. Cavalry came through Mesilla on its way south to insure "San Elizario was not taken over by aliens from Mexico," Howard returned to El Paso under the protection of the column. The following day, after eating luncheon at his hotel, Howard told his black servant, "I feel very restless and must have my revenge."[10] He then took a double-barreled shotgun, walked down the street, and entered a store where Cardis was sitting, having just finished writing a letter saying he hoped for peace in the area.

When Cardis saw Howard approaching he jumped up from his chair and tried to take refuge behind a tall bookkeeper's desk. The desk, however, covered only the upper part of his body and Howard, from about forty feet away, fired under the desk, hitting Cardis in the abdomen. Cardis then staggered

Luis Cardis (*l.*), legislator and political leader of the Mexican-American citizens of El Paso County, was shot to death by Charles Howard (*r.*). Howard was later killed by the mob at San Elizario. (Pioneer Association of El Paso, Texas)

backward, exposing his breast, and received Howard's second shot in the heart. Howard then calmly left the store, and shortly thereafter returned to Mesilla, New Mexico, unmolested.

Not satisfied with having escaped unpunished for this flagrant murder, Howard was still determined to retake possession of the salt lakes. Several months later, in early December 1877, flanked by a dozen of his own gunmen, Howard joined a detachment of Texas Rangers headed for the El Paso area. He had heard that a wagon train, loaded with salt from the lakes, was arriving there, and he wanted to start legal action to repossess the cargo. When the Rangers and Howard arrived, they received numerous warnings that their lives would be in danger from the irate Mexicans. Disregarding any advice, they continued on to San Elizario and the county seat.

## Let Me Die

There, menaced by a gathering mob, they were forced to hole up in the single-storied adobe building the Rangers used as a headquarters. But, since Lieutenant John B. Tays, the Ranger officer, had earlier sent a message to Fort Bayard requesting U.S. cavalrymen as reinforcements, the group was not unduly worried.

That night, a Wednesday, Charles Ellis went out into the dark streets of San Elizario. Some witnesses said he was trying to reason with the mob and deflect any violence; others reported that he was discovered eavesdropping in an attempt to learn how serious his friend Howard's situation might be. Regardless of the circumstances, he was seized by some Mexicans, tied, and dragged behind a horse while begging for his life. A crowd, said to number at least several hundred, watched as he was then stabbed to death, his throat cut for good measure, and his body thrown into a nearby *acequia*.[11] The bloodletting had begun.

The next morning, when the twenty-odd men in the Ranger's quarters looked out the windows, they found themselves surrounded by three concentric rings of armed Mexican pickets. Then the shots began to fly. In short order, Ranger Sergeant C. E. Mortimer was shot down in the street where he had been on sentry duty. Lieutenant Tays bravely walked out under fire, picked up the body, and brought it inside.

Throughout the day intermittent fire from the Hispanics sent bullets crashing through the door and windows of the building. Inside, the besieged men awaited the soldiers from Fort Bayard, not knowing that when the troops had arrived at the outskirts of San Elizario the night before their captain, either through stupidity or fear, had turned back with his fourteen men after having been told by the Mexican-American ringleader of the mob, Chico Barela, that there was no problem there.

It was at this point that John Atkinson entered the picture. Once again he proved to be at the wrong place at the wrong time. He had recently sold his store in San Elizario and planned to leave the village. But he had been a few days too late in making his departure and now, as an American and a friend of Howard's, he felt he was in jeopardy himself. Fearful of what

## From Martyrs to Murderers

the mob might do, he decided to leave his home and join forces with the other Anglos. This was a deadly mistake.

Somehow he sneaked past all the Mexican pickets carrying a small but heavy trunk which held his worldly possessions—eleven thousand dollars in specie, drafts, and notes, and other valuables. The moment he banged on the door of the Ranger's adobe stronghold and was admitted, he had sealed his fate.

The siege continued from Wednesday through Sunday, the Mexicans mounting assaults and the fatigued Rangers repulsing them. Howard had offered to give himself up to save the lives of the others, but Lieutenant Tays would not hear of it. Finally, on Monday morning, after the exhausted Rangers had agreed to a cease-fire and negotiations, the Mexicans promised, "If Howard gives himself up and gives up all claim to the salt lakes, no harm will come to him."[12]

Howard shook hands all around, smiled, and left the building to surrender. Lieutenant Tays insisted on accompanying him. Neither man, however, was fluent in Spanish, so they soon sent back for Atkinson to come and translate while they talked to the mob leaders. John Atkinson offered to turn over his eleven thousand dollars to the Mexicans if they allowed him, Howard, a Mr. Frank McBride, and the Rangers to depart unmolested. After much discussion the ringleaders agreed, providing Howard also promised to leave the area forever, and the Rangers surrendered to them. Chico Barela swore by the Holy Cross that he would faithfully keep his part of the agreement and John Atkinson told him, "Well, you've received a better price for us than you'd have got at public auction."[13]

The gringos, believing this to be the best solution, complied and were made prisoners. This was the only group, in the history of the Texas Rangers, to surrender.

However, one militant faction of the outraged salt users, unhappy with the agreement, decided Howard must die for the murder of their friend, Cardis. Soon a dozen or so came to the building where the captives were being held, hustled Howard outside, and lined up a firing squad. Unable to communicate with them in Spanish, Howard recognized the futility of further action, braced himself, and gave the command to fire. As he fell, one of the mob ran up with his machete and aimed a blow at Howard's face. The dying man twisted away at that moment and the attacker chopped off two of his own toes. Others, however, rushed forward to hack and chop at the body.

John Atkinson and Frank McBride were brought out next. Over the objections of Chico Barela who had made the bargain with Atkinson for his money, they, too, were lined up before the impromptu firing squad.

McBride, looking dazed and sad, said nothing. Atkinson, however, spoke up boldly in his excellent Spanish, reminding the mob of the pledges that had been made to release the party, pledges sworn by the Catholic men on the Holy Cross.

"Will you violate your oath?" he demanded.[14]

The bloodthirsty crowd shouted, "*Acabanlos! Acabanlos!*" ("Finish them! Finish them!")

Atkinson asked, "Then there is no remedy?"

"No! No!" shouted the crowd.

"Then let me die with honor. I will give the word."

With that, 'Limpin' John' Atkinson took off his coat and vest, opened his shirt baring his breast, and looked at his executioners. He said calmly, "When I give the word fire at my heart.....Fire!"

At the command, five bullets crashed into his belly. He staggered but did not fall.

"Higher!" he screamed. "*Mas arriba, cabrones!*" ("Higher, you bastards!")

Two more shots were fired. Atkinson fell but still he was not dead. The wounded man feebly pointed to his head and one of the firing party came forward and put the final bullet into his brain. At thirty-nine, Atkinson's life was over. McBride was killed instantly. The rabble now seemed sated and the blood bath was over. The two bodies were dragged away with ropes tied to horsemen's saddles. They were stripped and mutilated and later found in an old well half a mile away.

Then the crowd fell to looting. Within forty-eight hours thirty thousand dollars worth of money and goods had disappeared across the river to Mexico. The ringleaders then turned

## From Martyrs to Murderers

### STATE OF TEXAS.

*San Elizario Nov 31, 187*

I Hereby Certify, That C. E. Mortimer a Sargent of Captain Sparks Company ( "A" ) of the Frontier Battalion, was mustered into the State Service on the 11th day of November 1877. The said C. E. Mortimer has pay due him from November the 11th to the present date.

There is due said C. E. Mortimer the sum of 26 66/100 Dollars. He is indebted to the State of Texas 3 70/100 Dollars, on account of Order of C. E. Ellis

Balance 22 80/100

Approved: $

1st Lt. J. B. Tays
Commanding Company.

Adjutant General.

Received of _____ this _____ day of _____ 187_, _____ Dollars in full of the above account.

(Signed in Duplicate.)

This pay voucher was made out to Sergeant C.E. Mortimer and signed by Charles Ellis and Lieutenant J.B. Tays on November 31, 1877. None of them could have known that less than two weeks later both Ellis and Mortimer would be dead and Tays marked as the only Texas Ranger ever to surrender his command.
(Texas State Archives)

loose the other civilian prisoners. Finally, they brought out the Ranger's horses and told them to mount and ride out of town. Undaunted, Lieutenant Tays spoke up, saying, "In the name of the State of Texas I demand our arms."[15] The Mexicans, however, gave him nothing more than an escort as far as the neighboring town of Ysleta.

American retaliation was not long in coming. A short time later detachments of soldiers, Tays and his Rangers, and a civilian posse re-invaded San Elizario.

Although a few of the guilty were caught and punished, most escaped into Mexico where a wall of silence protected them. Even though rewards were offered for the leaders, no Mexican ever turned a finger to collect the money. Frustrated in their search for vengeance, some of the Americans committed outrages upon innocent residents which were as heinous as those they were trying to revenge.

For many years there was great bitterness on both sides of the Rio Grande. Occasionally an American with business across the river saw a family happily riding by with Atkinson's horse and buggy but, with great discretion, ignored the matter.

'Limpin' John' Atkinson had his faults but, in the words of one newspaper reporter, "He died as he had lived—a brave man."[16] Perhaps this should be his epitaph.

Endnotes:

[1] John G. Atkinson military service records, National Archives, Washington, D.C. and 1870 El Paso County, Texas, Census.

[2] The New Mexico volunteer organizations, made up mostly of Hispanics who were illiterate in English, were anxious to obtain soldiers who could read and write the language in which the U.S. Army operated. They often arranged these transfers of willing Anglos from both the Regular Army and California Volunteers and, in most cases, immediately promoted the men into positions of responsibility.

[3] Ernest Marchand, ed., *News From Fort Craig, New Mexico, 1863. Civil War Letters of Andrew Ryan, with the First California Volunteers* (Santa Fe: Stagecoach Press, 1966), pp. 48-49, 63-64.

[4] John G. Atkinson military pension records, National Archives, Washington, D.C.

[5] Lt. George H. Pettis, Co. F, 1st New Mexico Volunteers, to Lt. R. Hudson, Post Adjutant, Fort Craig, May 9, 1865, Record Group 94, "Records of the Adjutant General's Office, 1783-1917," Regimental Record Books, 1st Regiment, New Mexico Infantry, Letters Sent and Received and Orders, 1861-1866. One officer was reported to have been "providentially saved after being in the water a long time. Three men of Co. F supported him until relief reached them." The bodies of several of the soldiers were not recovered until a week later.

[6] Invalid Pension Claim, John G. Atkinson Pension Records, National Archives, Washington, D.C.

[7] *Santa Fe New Mexican*, June 30, 1868.

[8] W.W. Mills, *Forty Years at El Paso* (Chicago: Press of W.B. Conkey Company, 1901), pp. 122-23. Further proof that Atkinson made some political enemies can be found among the papers in Atkinson's military pension file in Washington. In the summer of 1872, John Atkinson initiated a request for a pension based upon the disability engendered by the shattered hip. Included in his file is a letter signed only with the name 'Wash,' in which a resident of San Elizario has written to his own father (apparently in Washington) asking that he obtain, from the Commissioner of Pensions, the name of the parties who signed affidavits for Atkinson's pension request. The correspondent wrote, "He was not wounded in the line of his duty, but in a drunken spree, and away from his command." In reality, however, Atkinson had made no spurious claims in his application and, in addition, would not live long enough to secure his pension.

[9] C. L. Sonnichsen, *The El Paso Salt War* (El Paso: Texas Western Press, 1973), p. 22.

[10] C. L. Sonnichsen, *Pass of the North*, Vol. 1 (El Paso: Texas Western Press, 1968), p. 201.

[11] Irrigation ditch.

[12] Sonnichsen, *Pass of the North*, p. 207.

[13] Robert J. Casey, *The Texas Border* (New York: The Bobbs-Merrill Co., 1950), p. 148.

[14] Sonnichsen, *The El Paso Salt War*, p. 56.

[15] Ibid., p. 57.

[16] *The Mesilla Independent*, December 22, 1877.

# A Plethora of Purple Prose

There it was, on the front page, for the whole town to see! The article in the *Silver City* (New Mexico) *Enterprise* said:

> Quite a serious accident happened to Messrs. Morehead and Whitehill the two heavy-weight democratic candidates. They found the water much deeper in the Gila [River] than they had anticipated. Their buggy was tipped over and both men narrowly escaped with their lives. The accident proved to be a real calamity as two large demijohns of democratic whiskey were lost in the water. The latest report from the Gila states that the suckers are not all dead yet. In justice to these gentlemen it should be stated that it is the first time in many years that they have been known to take water. It is hoped that an incident of this kind may never occur again.[1]

Territorial newspapers! What a colorful, subjective, and fascinating mixed bag of historical information they contained, particularly in the earlier days of their publication.

(*above*) When a mining boom town burst onto the scene, it soon had a newspaper, even if it had to be set up temporarily in the open air as the *Kingston Shaft* was done in 1886. (Museum of New Mexico) (*below*) Unplastered adobe walls and poor lighting did not deter these early Socorro, New Mexico, typesetters from getting their work done. (Author's Collection)

## Purple Prose

Local editions usually carried a few, somewhat belated, international and national items gleaned from Eastern papers, via correspondence, or over the telegraph. The remainder of the periodical was normally given over to political, military, mining, or Indian news, depending upon the region in which it was published. But the most arresting pieces were the human interest stories. Given a murder, an elopement, a tragedy or scandal of some sort, Territorial journalists could and would supply some of the most lurid, gossipy, opinionated and judgmental prose a scandal sheet reader could hope for.

No one's personal business was sacred or off limits to the editors. In 1886, one New Mexico newspaper, under the headline of "Marry the Gal, or Else," published the following item:

> Last Saturday night an attorney and a deputy sheriff arrived here from northeast Missouri, with a requisition for M. F. Bailey, a well-known bank clerk, who has been here nearly a year. The result was that he left with them next morning, and is not expected to return. The officers stated that he would certainly be prosecuted unless he compromised the case by becoming the husband to a girl to whom he was once engaged.[2]

Good taste was obviously not a prerequisite for membership in the Territorial fourth estate. After the death of a well-known and much respected citizen of Santa Fe, his rapidly escalating descent into madness was graphically described in the local press under the guise of sympathetic regret. The article said:

> ...Last summer his mind began to give evident signs of becoming inflicted with insanity. He had ever been noted in this city for his sober industry and rather studious habits. He was regarded as a man of punctilious veracity and business integrity.... Rather early in the summer he began to exhibit an excessive egotism, founded upon an impression that he was a

man of great astronomical genius and had invented a kind of solar compass surpassing anything before known in simplicity and accuracy. He believed the invention would yield him immense wealth. He then passed to the impression that he owned gold mines fabulous in value. Diamonds and all precious stones filled his possessions. Santa Fe was shortly to receive, on account of his mines, a population exceeding New York. His hallucinations then took another turn. He announced himself the second Savior that had been sent to the Jews. His mind then turned to a political wildness. He proclaimed New Mexico a state, and federal authority ended here. Contended he was President of the Republic and gave orders, verbally and in writing, to civil and military officers, and upon finding himself not obeyed, he declared them removed. Finally, it was thought best to confine him, for he became violent and dangerous from his temper. His brother then made excellent arrangements for his removal to an asylum in the states to be treated. On the road he died.[3]

Not infrequently, editors of Territorial newspapers placed themselves just one step below God. Publicly, and in print, they passed premature judgment on the guilt or innocence, mental condition, or motives of a wide variety of citizens, without, apparently, any misgivings or fear of libel suits. Although, in a few cases, inflamed victims of their vitriolic pens were known to challenge them to a duel.

Take, for example, the pre-trial piece which the editor of the *Las Vegas Daily Optic* ran in his April 15, 1881, issue. Not only was he willing to publish an article written by a correspondent who signed himself "A Vigilante," but he also embellished it with an inflammatory headline inscribed in ridiculous alliteration to make it more eye-catching:

# Purple Prose

## Refugee Refugio
### A Rollicking and Revolting Record of Robbery and Rapine
### The Wife Killing Mania Brings a Fiend to Justice

Tramperos, April 11. Sheriff Mason Bowman of Springer reached here today on his way to that place with one Refugio Maes as his travelling companion. He was well secured in iron harness and was keenly guarded by the official, who evidently meant that by no manner of accident should he escape. This Refugio Maes has a record of which, as a criminal, he has reason to feel proud. It may be that his crimes may not have been numerous, those known against him have been of the most brutal and revolting character, and it seems indeed strange that an individual of his stripe would be allowed to run at large so long as he has.

The crime for which Sheriff Bowman has arrested him, (on the strength of a true bill placed against him at the last Cimarron court) is that of killing his wife, which dastardly deed he accomplished over a year ago, whilst residing near the Tramperos.

It appears that she was his second wife and that he had disposed of number one in a summary manner, a few years previously, but in another locality.

For the first offense he seems never to have been brought to trial, a fact which no doubt encouraged him very much in going into wife killing as a regular business. It would really seem as if he married but to kill, for the unfortunate girl whom he butchered on the Tramperos, had been his wife only a few weeks, and shortly after her unhappy death he sought another woman as his wife.

The murder was committed in the most cold-blooded manner, and has no equal in this country for its brutality. It appears that the girl was only thirteen years of age, was employed one day preparing meat to be cooked for dinner, when the fiend asked her if she would like to die with him, supposing, presumably, that she fancied him jesting, she replied in the affirmative, whereupon he stabbed her with a knife and then, taking the tomahawk from her hands, he chopped her almost to pieces. She finally made her way out of the *jickal*[4] [sic] and fell dead on the ground, gashed and mangled in a horrifying manner.

The neighbors had the body of the unfortunate woman interred, the murderer refusing to assist in any manner in the sad ceremony, at which he simply laughed. I had almost forgotten to state that after destroying his wife he made a very wild attempt upon his own life, drawing a knife carefully across his throat he inflicted a slight wound, and then ceased his suicidal effort on the score that "it hurt too much."

### Paying Money For Blood.

The father and brother of the deceased woman resided in the vicinity, but they made no attempt to have the murderer brought to justice, and it transpired afterwards that one hundred dollars judiciously distributed by Maes had healed the wounded feelings of the girl's relatives. However, to make a long story short, it may be stated that Maes was subsequently arrested and underwent a preliminary trial at which he was committed to be tried for murder, but while on his way to Mora jail he was rescued by a mob. This was close on to a year ago and since then he has been at large without any effort to re-arrest him. The moment Sheriff Bowman received the warrant for his arrest, however, he set out, and overhauled his man.... When told that he was a prisoner he made no reply but stoutly refused the operation of adjusting the manacles and shackles. He threatened to kill the Sheriff at the first favorable opportunity, but it is not likely that this favorable opportunity will ever be afforded him. When asked why he killed his wife, he coolly replied, because he wanted to, that he did not wish to live with her and did not wish any other man to live with her. A forcible argument which should enable an intelligent jury to come to a verdict without much trouble.

### The Insanity Dodge

The plea of insanity will be raised at the trial, but my opinion is that he is a fiend and not a fool. At all events, if he is insane his place is within the walls of an asylum, and if not insane, the county can surely afford the necessary hemp to swing him into kingdom come.

# Purple Prose

> Such characters as he have no business at large in a civilized community, and the sooner he is dealt with the better. He will be tried at Springer and committed.

None of that "innocent until proven guilty" foolishness for this correspondent! It would seem, after the publication of this piece, that a trial would be redundant.

The term "alleged" apparently was missing from the dictionaries of many editors of Territorial dailies or weeklies. They were men of strong and sure convictions, and murderers, or at least those accused of the crime, supplied an excellent opportunity to trot out all the attention-demanding, impassioned adjectives and derogatory nouns which seemed to be the stock in trade of both the news media and the pulpit in those days.

A typical story appeared in the *New Mexican* of May 28, 1875, in the form of a letter to the editor from the northern town of Abiquiu. It read:

> One of the most cruel and bloodthirsty murders ever committed in this Territory was perpetrated at Coyote, a new settlement, distant twenty miles from this place, on Monday the 17th.
>
> A boy named Evaristo Gallegos, about sixteen-years-old, tried to commit an outrage on a young girl aged twelve named Maritana Martin, and not being able to accomplish his hellish act, he deliberately went and loaded an old Army musket and shot the poor girl through the back, the ball entering near the spine and coming out of the left of her breast, she died in a few minutes afterward in great agony, having, however, had time to tell her mother and others present the particulars of the outrage. She was nursing an infant sister at the time, which was severely wounded in the arm, and having fractured its skull in falling against a wall with the deceased, the child is in a dangerous state. The murderer is still at large, having taken to the mountains after committing the terrible act. I am afraid that the authorities are making but slight effort to hunt him up. It is the duty of all good citizens to assist the local authorities to catch the scoundrel and bring him to justice; a warning to evil doers.

# From Martyrs to Murderers

Charles P. Clever was maligned by the editor/owner of a Santa Fe newspaper whose political loyalties lay with Clever's opponents. (Museum of New Mexico)

It was not just in the area of violent crimes that the newspaper owners and editors acted as judge and jury. The publications were, of course, extremely influential political tools, and partisanship was the order of the day. Innuendo, insinuation, and allusion were commonly used against political foes and, if they did not work, outright lies were occasionally printed. The battles were often bitter, and any weapon, no matter how ignoble, was used.

When Charles Clever won a hotly-contested race for New Mexico's territorial delegate to Congress in 1867 and took his seat in Washington in the autumn, the *Santa Fe New Mexican*, a Republican newspaper which had backed his opponent, continued to malign him. The election was being contested, and the *New Mexican's* editor continued to try to sway public opinion. He picked up a small item from the *Washington Chronicle* in which an Eastern reporter referred to Clever as "a certain Spanish gentleman." Apparently the journalist assumed anyone representing New Mexico would be Hispanic.

With a clever distortion of the truth and a noxious pen, the editor managed to combine religious prejudice, character assassination, and the question of patriotic loyalties into a beautiful example of the worst in partisan journalism. He wrote:

> Really, New Mexico, we should say, ought to feel proud of its *sitting* Delegate. Apostate Jew, and now a Catholic; occupying a seat in Congress that belongs to another, and at last abjuring not only his "fatherland," but the country of his adoption, and all of a sudden turning *Spaniard*; really, Clever is a trump of which New Mexico ought to feel proud.... However, the mess of potage for which he sold his religion in this country, he now enjoys...we think it proper to say to our friends in Washington, to whom Clever is a Spaniard, that when he came to New Mexico, some fifteen years ago, he was a German of the Hebrew persuasion, and though he did drop off the mantle of Hebraic faith, we were not aware until the little affair in Washington...that he became a Spaniard by throwing off his mixed German origin.[4]

The Native Americans, of course, were condemned almost universally; designated by the most disparaging labels and accused, often without proof, of heinous crimes. After all, there was a war going on and they were the adversary. Like other societies, who, during periods of conflict, depict their enemies as atrocity-ridden wild beasts while minimizing wrongdoing on their own part, the European-Americans used inflammatory language, epithets, and abusive phrases when writing about the Indians.

In some instances, with great temerity, journalists also made psychological, legal, and moral judgments on whole lives in single paragraphs. For example:

> We learn that Pino, who killed Schwarzkopf, was buried without benefit of clergy. The belief having obtained that while he was very likely partially insane when he committed the murder; that the enormity of the offense aroused him to a sense of his situation and that he killed himself rather than submit to the penalty of the law, where the case was so overwhelmingly against him. The Catholic Church, according to their laws, refusing service to a voluntary suicide. He was a cattle thief.[6]

# From Martyrs to Murderers

And that, it must be assumed, was the final and definitive word on the late, lamented Mr. Pino.

Of course, not all the items were depressing, gory, or unfair. There were flashes of humor, as in the small item which stated, "Somebody lifted the body of a porker out of Gen. Proudfit's corral last night without consulting his wishes. They were considerate enough to leave the head and legs." And also the piece about Indians which said, "The first thing an enlightened citizen of this country does on waking up in the morning is to feel for his hair, and then look in his corral for his stock and moccasin tracks."[7]

And finally, no one can deny that some articles were educational in the extreme. For every person who ever wondered how it felt to be scalped, the *Santa Fe Weekly Gazette* had an answer. A former soldier, Delos G. Sandbertson, related the tale of how his hair was lifted at the Battle of Washita. It was reported thus:

> I was in the infantry. Custer had command of the troops. There was quite a force of cavalry with us, they were about a mile in the rear when we first discovered the reds.... The reds were encamped in a sort of valley, and we were within eighteen rods of them for a half an hour before daybreak. Just in the gray of the morning the firing commenced on both sides, and we had it all our own way for a few minutes, the cursed snakes being much confused and not knowing which way was up. At length they rallied and we could hear Black Kettle shouting and ordering. The vermin got into holes and behind rocks—any-where they could find a place, and begin to fight back with a will. We fired whenever we could see a topknot, and shot squaws— there were lots of them—just as quick as Indians. We just went in for wiping out the whole gang. When it was fairly daylight, we all gave a big yell and charged right down into the camp. The lodges were all standing yet, and lots of Indians in them. As we run through the alleys, a big red jumped out at me from behind a

tent, and before I could shorten up enough to run him through with my bayonet, a squaw grabbed me around the legs and twisted me down. The camp was then full of men fighting, and everybody seemed yelling as loud as he could. When I fell, I went over backward, dropping my gun, I had just got part ways up again, the squaw yanking me by the hair, when the Indian clubbed my gun and struck me across the neck. He might just have well run me through but he wasn't used to the bayonet or didn't think. The blow stunned me; it didn't hurt in the least, but gave me a numb feeling all over. I couldn't have gotten to my feet then if all alone, while the squaw kept screeching and pulling my hair out by handfuls.

I heard some of our boys shouting close by, and the squaw started and ran—one of the boys killing her not three rods off. The Indian stepped one foot on my chest, and with his hand gathered up the hair near the crown of my head. He wasn't very tender about it, but jerked my head this way and that, and pinched like Satan. My eyes were partially opened, and I could see the beadwork and trimming on his leggins. Suddenly I felt the awfulest biting, cutting flash go round my head, and then it seemed as if my whole head had been jerked clean off. I never felt such pain in all my life; why, it was like pulling your brains right out. I didn't know anything more for two or three days and when I came to, to find that I had the sorest head of any human that lived. If the boys killed the viper they didn't get back my scalp, perhaps it got lost in the snow. I was shipped down to Laramie after a bit, and all the nursing I got hain't made the hair grow out on this spot yet.[8]

'Now that's a lively first-person account capable of allowing any reader to experience vicariously an event not likely to occur during his lifetime!

# From Martyrs to Murderers

Endnotes:

[1] *Silver City Enterprise*, October 8, 1886.
[2] Ibid., October 1, 1886.
[3] *Santa Fe New Mexican*, November 21, 1863.
[4] A *jacal* is a Mexican word for a roughly built shack or hut made of brush or adobe.
[5] Ibid., October 21, 1868.
[6] Ibid., May 24, 1875.
[7] Ibid., May 18, 1875; December 8, 1864.
[8] *Santa Fe Weekly Gazette*, July 24, 1869. The item originally appeared in the *Detroit Press* and was apparently reprinted in the *Gazette* because New Mexicans, who had much experience in Indian fighting, would probably find it of interest. However, some of the details in this account are historically suspect, raising the question of whether Sandbertson was really at Washita.

# Hillsboro's Scandalous Sadie

It has been half a century since Sadie Orchard took her last breath, but she is still achieving, in death, what she strove so hard to get in life—attention, admiration, celebrity, and notoriety. Formerly one of the most colorful and outrageous women in Territorial New Mexico, Sarah Jane 'Sadie' Creech Orchard is having the last laugh on her critics—the more respectable citizens of the towns of Kingston and Hillsboro, New Mexico—who are now forgotten by history.

As a result of her secrecy, deliberate misrepresentations, and imaginative role playing while alive, it is difficult to separate fact from fiction when researching Sadie's life but, nonetheless, her story is a tantalizing one.

Even Sadie's beginnings are shrouded in mystery. That she was born in England seems well established, but her birth date is not. In 1900 Sadie informed a census worker that she was born in August 1861. Sadie's gravestone, however, will forever proclaim that she was four years younger; possibly as she aged she eliminated years for vanity's sake.

## From Martyrs to Murderers

This uncertainty is representative of Sadie Orchard's whole life. Trying to define her is impossible; she is as elusive as quicksilver—a paradox. In fact, at the core of her being, Sadie herself seemed unsure of who and what she really was.

She was a prostitute and a madam, but initiated a drive to raise money to build a church and used her vigor and stamina to achieve many charitable works. She tried, in dress and customs, to imitate the aristocratic British upper-class, but then talked and acted as vulgarly as any longshoreman. She adored feminine frills but delighted in outdoing men at men's work. She was reviled and she was loved. She was also a hard-nosed businesswoman, but yearned to play the role of the pampered, genteel lady, and although she desperately wanted the acceptance of the town's "proper" citizens, Sadie's natural exuberance and earthiness stood in the way of ever really obtaining it.

Some accounts state that Sadie learned her wicked ways as a young woman around the London docks, but Sadie's official version was that she came to the United States as a nine-year-old. One El Paso journalist wrote, even while Sadie was still alive, that she and her husband had been running a stage line in the area in 1872. This is an example of the many unreliable stories in existence. In 1872 Sadie would have been only eleven years old!

Sadie's first documented appearance in southwestern New Mexico took place in the mountain mining town of Kingston shortly after its boom. In late 1882, the discovery of a chunk of extremely rich silver ore near the south end of the Black Range set off an excitement that resulted in the formation of the town. In a matter of only weeks, more than eighteen hundred men and a few women had moved in and established what would become the richest silver producing area in New Mexico in the nineteenth century.

According to Sadie, by the time she moved to Kingston it had a population of five thousand and "...a big silver boom going full sway. Dance halls and saloons did a rushing business almost day and night. Fortunes were made, and in some cases, lost over night."[1] Always the entrepreneur, Sadie arrived and set up a house of prostitution on a street called Virtue Avenue.

Whenever possible, Sadie applied her personal standards to the girls she had working in her cribs. She tried to obtain the prettiest women available and made them dress in her version of high fashion. Sadie knew what the miners, prospectors, and cowboys wanted, and by presenting a "superior" product she was able to beat out much of the competition and command good prices.

In her youth Sadie was reputed to be a real beauty. She was particularly proud of her tiny waist and feet, her lovely cornflower-blue eyes, and her creamy English complexion. All this was enhanced by jet-black hair and her stylish finery and jewelry. In one instance she was described as "...a tiny, high-bosomed woman with short feet in shorter shoes...and a wicked chuckle to punctuate her obscenities and profanities."[2] She loved to imitate the fashion and actions of the British upper-crust and was successful in looking the part, but only for brief periods. The moment Sadie opened her mouth the proverbial cat was out of the bag. Her atrocious Cockney accent, combined with a vocabulary profane enough to make a sailor blush, gave her away as a product of the meanest streets of London's Limehouse district.

When the initial rush to stake claims and snatch a share of the riches subsided, Kingston settled down. As the tents and whipsaw-lumber structures were replaced by more permanent buildings, residents realized that, although the town had twenty-two saloons and numerous brothels, it was without a single place of worship. In a trite but apparently true tale, it is said that Sadie and her "girls" canvassed the entire community soliciting money to build one. Sadie set the example by donating her own diamond lavaliere. Her efforts raised fifteen hundred dollars from the miners, gamblers, and local inhabitants, enough to erect a small stone church.

At some point during this period, the famed Lillian Russell's troupe of actors came to perform in Kingston. Years later an elderly woman would reminisce saying, "the only reason Miss Russell came to town was to visit Sadie Orchard...rumor had it that she and Lillian used to act on the stage together on the

West Coast."³ If Sadie herself is to be believed, the story is completely untrue, but Sadie's colorful nature seemed to spawn such rumors.⁴

Her marital status, while plying one of the world's oldest trades in Kingston, is another item for speculation. Again, numerous versions exist. If statements she made to the census taker years later were true, then Sadie would have been married at the time. Other sources, however, claim that she married James W. Orchard in an attempt to achieve respectability only after having been an extremely active and popular prostitute.⁵

It was rumored that Sadie romanced "nearly every man in every [mining] camp" in the area, but this is undoubtedly a gross exaggeration.⁶ The fact is, however, that the combination of free-spending miners, Sadie's exciting personality and her good business sense resulted in a quick accumulation of wealth for the lively, pretty woman. She soon indulged herself in finery and jewelry, but also was generous in staking prospectors and loaning or even giving away money.

Sadie's chosen mate was so overshadowed by his dynamic, vivid wife that today even his name seems to have faded away. He is so obscure that articles and stories cannot agree on his name; he is listed as L. W., J. W., S. J., Harry, Mr. Orchard, or simply "Sadie's husband." The gentleman's lack of drive, initiative and determination, however, have been liberally referred to. In short order, Sadie literally and figuratively took over the reins of his stagecoach business, which she then operated for fourteen years.

The rolling stock consisted of two red and yellow Concord coaches and a freight wagon. The line transported passengers and freight between Kingston, Hillsboro, and Lake Valley – three gold and silver mining boom towns in their heyday. Along with the shipments and the business travelers, the line also transported passengers on their way to visit 'Tugboat Annie,' 'Missouri Lil,' 'Big Sal,' 'Rosarita' or other "chippies" on Virtue Avenue. Either way, Sadie made money. One author has said that while, in theory, Sadie's husband ran the stage line "there was never any question as to the identity of the senior partner of the enterprise."⁷

# Hillsboro's Scandalous Sadie

(*above*) Sadie Orchard gained much renown driving the 'Mountain Pride' stagecoach down rugged mountain trails. (George T. miller Photo, Museum of New Mexico) (*below*) These ladies of Kingston certainly knew who Sadie was, but probably never socialized with her. (J.C. Burge photo, Museum of New Mexico)

Sadie, not content with just overseeing operations, had to flaunt convention and prove something to herself so, tiny as she was, she often drove the great Concord coach. The incorrigible Sadie, perched in the high driver's seat, reins in hand, would guide the teams of four and sometimes six horses and the heavy, lumbering coach through Box Canyon and down steep mountain trails so narrow that the sides of the vehicle occasionally rubbed against outcroppings. "I could kick the foot brake with the best of them," Sadie bragged with a laugh years later.[8]

The Lake Valley, Hillsboro, and Kingston Stage Line, also known as the LVH & K, or just Orchard's Mountain Pride, left Kingston and followed a seven-mile-long route of canyon cliffs and bottoms, through narrow defiles, sometimes over rocks or deep sand, and sometimes through flooding, to Hillsboro. After picking up passengers there it traveled twenty miles to Lake Valley, stopping en route at two relay stations to change teams. The final thirteen-mile leg was to the settlement of Nutt, where the stage arrived in time to meet the train. It was forty miles of jolting over broken ground and hazardous trails, with one-hundred-pound Sadie, whip in hand and boot heel resting on the brake, very much in control!

On one occasion the stagecoach was ambushed by some Ojo Caliente Apaches. Another time bandits held up one of the stages which was transporting a shipment of $175,000, not an unheard of sum for an area where gold and silver mines were booming. Fortunately for Sadie she was not driving on either occasion, although she was probably disappointed at missing the excitement.

Many years later Sadie and spouse sold the stage line to Mr. Mister, a businessman known locally for the excellent wine he made. Some say the henpecked Orchard had turned to liquor for solace, others insist that Sadie's husband found driving the route too much work. Regardless of the reason, by 1902, Orchard was underbid and lost the mail contract. Without that source of income he was forced to sell the stage operation.

It was in those early years while living in Kingston that Sadie first met Albert Bacon Fall and Edward L. Doheny, two men who would later gain national notoriety through Washington's Teapot Dome Scandal when Fall was Secretary of the Interior and Doheny an extremely wealthy oil man. Both worked at the mines, "pounding a drill up in Kingston," according to Sadie.[9] Other early acquaintances later became millionaires as Texas oil men and gambling casino owners.

During that early bonanza period for New Mexico's Black Range, mine outputs flourished. From Kingston alone more than ten million dollars in rich pay dirt was extracted in a few years. Always the astute businesswoman, Sadie opened a second "sporting house" in nearby Hillsboro, a town circled by gold and silver mines that produced six million dollars worth of precious metals.

The most poignant story from the area is that of two miners who struck a vein and sold out for $100,000. Two days after the sale, the new owners, following a ten-inch stringer, suddenly burst into a chamber "as big as a house," and viewed, in awe, the silver-studded walls flashing in the lantern's beam. This subterranean cavity, named the Bridal Chamber, produced 2,500,000 ounces of silver, much of it horn silver so unadulterated it was sawed and cut into blocks instead of being blasted. At the time it was reported that some portions of the ore were so pure and porous a candle flame would melt them into globules. The Bridal Chamber was the richest, purest pocket of silver *ever* found *anywhere* in the world.[10]

But, like other boom and bust towns, within less than a decade Kingston began to feel the effects of depleted ore veins and its economy slowed. In 1886 Sadie moved her base of operations to Hillsboro, nine miles to the east. Hillsboro's broader-based population included cowboys and the soldiers stationed nearby to protect the area from Geronimo's still-active Apaches.

Now Sadie was really in her element. Aiming for respectability, she opened the Ocean Grove Hotel, which became known the width and length of New Mexico for its excellence. Travelers, from salesmen to politicians, and cattlemen to lawyers, arranged their schedules to spend the night in Hillsboro.

## From Martyrs to Murderers

The Ocean Grove offered everything a fellow could want—excellent food and drink, a clean bed, and, if desired, discrete female companionship on the side, for the ever-practical Sadie made sure that each of the hostelry's rooms had a convenient outside entrance.

One of Sadie's biggest assets was her Chinese cook, Tom Ying, famed for the sumptuous food he produced on his big, black, Banquet wood stove. She also kept a fine stock of imported liquors for those whose discriminating palates might reject the mundane intoxicants normally available. And, of course, Ying's handsome copper coffee urn turned out gallons of the second-favorite beverage in town.

Sadie was now prospering like never before. With the stage line and the hotel, most of her income was obtained from "morally acceptable" businesses. The old daydream of being "proper English gentry" dared raise its head and Sadie had elaborate riding habits made for herself. She dressed in ornate silks and satins, decked herself out in diamonds and a gold coin necklace, wore fine, butter-soft leather gloves, and topped the entire ensemble off with a high silk hat. Then out she went, riding sidesaddle, galloping over the countryside, accompanied by her hounds and with her hired lackey, a Black youngster she named 'Boots,' in attendance.

Sadie, caught up in her fantasy, was unaware that her behavior might look foolishly inappropriate in the rugged, isolated, hardscrabble area. Sadie was at the height of her glory. She was on a first-name basis with most of the politicians and men of wealth, both local and throughout the Territory, who often treated her like "one of the boys." Proof of this privileged status was discovered, after her death, in letters from many powerful men, including former governors, that showed she had dubbed them with pet names which they loved. Her bar and hotel were the center of all important activity in the area, so she was "in the know," and able to wield a certain amount of influence. There was only one thing more that Sadie wanted—to step over the line into respectability.

(*left*) Sadie, c. 1886, in her tall silk hat, butter-soft leather gloves, bouffant sleeves and bustled skirt, playing the fine lady. (Author's Collection)

(*below*) Even as she aged, Sadie retained some of the looks and style from her youth. (Jacob Posevich photo, Museum of New Mexico)

## From Martyrs to Murderers

Carried away by her successes, Sadie orchestrated a lovely "English garden party." At great effort and expense she had molded ices imported quite a distance from El Paso. Lovely engraved invitations were sent out and dainty finger sandwiches made. But, as the day approached, it became obvious that the local fathers, who numbered Sadie among their friends, were extremely reluctant to send their children to the festivities. What sort of blackmail Sadie resorted to is not known, but one way or another she managed to recruit a reasonable attendance, enough at any rate, to save face.

In 1899, Hillsboro's courthouse became the site of a murder trial for one of New Mexico's most intriguing, and still celebrated, criminal cases. This was an exciting time for Sadie. National attention was drawn to the little town in the mountains of southwestern New Mexico. A telegraph line, Hillsboro's first, was strung many miles through the mountains to facilitate national media coverage of the spectacular event.

The case revolved around the mysterious disappearance, three years earlier, of Colonel Albert J. Fountain and his young son, Henry. Although the bodies of Fountain, a notable, powerful, and wealthy judge, and his child were never discovered, several equally wealthy and powerful men were accused of their murders.

Hillsboro had never seen such a furor, nor had it ever been so crowded. Lawyers, politicians, newsmen, supporters for both sides, and the just-plain-curious jammed into town, straining the facilities. Obviously the hotels were unable to serve all those in attendance; just in witnesses alone there were seventy-five—half for the prosecution and half for the defense. To keep order and handle the throng, two tent camps were set up to house the adversarial witnesses, one at the north end of town, the other on the south.[11]

Only the most favored were fortunate enough to have rooms at Sadie's hotel. Her sympathies were obviously with the defendants, who arranged to have Tom Ying's culinary wonders prepared and sent to their cells at the Hillsboro jail. After their acquittal, it was to Sadie's Ocean Grove that they trooped, where an extravagant celebration was held.

## Hillsboro's Scandalous Sadie

As the festivities were taking place at the hotel, Sadie's stage line generated big profits. That evening, after the not guilty verdict was brought in, demand for passage out of town was high. Newsmen, spectators, and even witnesses like famed Lincoln County Sheriff Pat Garrett, wanted to leave the crowded community. Although normal coach capacity was nine passengers, that night Sadie's driver managed to cram on and into the vehicle a record number, a whopping twenty-three![12]

As the years passed, discord between Sadie and the almost invisible Mr. Orchard accelerated. The final straw was Orchard's failure to win renewal of the mail contract, which, in turn, led to the sale of the stage line to Fred W. Mister. At Sadie's demand, Orchard left hearth and home permanently, some say while being peppered by buckshot launched by his irate spouse.

Sadie, Tom Ying, and Hillsboro, however, were teamed for life. Tom, the "maestro" of the culinary, with his black skull cap and grocery lists written in cryptic Oriental characters, was a local personality almost as well known as Sadie. Tom, who had an irrational fear of shears, allowed no one but Sadie to cut his hair.

As the years passed and Sadie aged, she mellowed and became less flamboyant. She continued operating her businesses, but World War I had a dampening effect on the economy in Hillsboro. Then, in 1918, came the terrible scourge of influenza, and even remote, isolated Hillsboro was not spared. Sadie swung into action once again, "doubling for whatever was needed: doctor, nurse, hospital, or undertaker."[13] Never one to expect others to do what she would not do herself, Sadie rolled up her sleeves and pitched in. She cooked and cleaned and sat up nights with the sick. She scrubbed clothes, wiped fevered brows, and sympathized with the mourning. She cut up her silk and velvet gowns for cloth to line children's coffins, and, when needed, used her own buggy to transport them up the steep hill to the cemetery. On the graves she placed blooms cut from the plants growing in her dining room window.[14]

# From Martyrs to Murderers

In addition, this woman, whose speech was still punctuated with profanities, found homes for orphans created by the epidemic. She supported more than one family whose breadwinner was dead or in prison, and earned the gratitude of most townspeople, who now saw beyond her unpolished exterior.

A few years later, Sadie, still an entrepreneur, made and sold bootleg whiskey from her basement. Throughout Prohibition Sadie had an unblemished record; she was never raided or charged by local, state, or federal agents. It was common knowledge that Sadie had "the goods" on enough powerful men to assure her undisturbed traffic.

The only man who ever got the best of Sadie was Old Man Time himself. As the years passed, Hillsboro lost its county seat status, the mines were played out, and the town remained small and isolated. Sadie's money and influence slowly melted away and she became little more than a local curiosity; someone to be interviewed about once a decade by regional newspaper reporters in need of a little feature story about the lady stage driver. She and Tom Ying were growing old together in quiet Hillsboro.

In 1943, somewhere in the vicinity of her eightieth year, Sadie died. A World War was in progress, so little attention was given to the event. Surprisingly, Sadie was not laid to rest in Hillsboro, but, instead, many miles away in Hot Springs, the new county seat.[15] Tom Ying, who remained a local personality for what seemed like eons, died in 1957. His age was reported to be somewhere between 104 and 116 years. He is still in Hillsboro, resting in the old cemetery on the western edge of town.

Sadie's estate was meager. The only item of any real value she had been able to hold onto was her gold coin necklace. The sale of her possessions brought only a few dollars and after the funeral expenses were paid a balance of only forty-five dollars remained.

But Sadie's real legacy was the addition of an exciting, colorful figure to New Mexico history, and a number of intriguing questions. Did Sadie really ride down Hillsboro's main street "a

## Hillsboro's Scandalous Sadie

la Lady Godiva" to win a bet?[16] Very possibly. Were the intentions lethal or humorous when she and a girlfriend set off a charge of dynamite under the chair occupied by that friend's husband? Again, who knows? And there is the haunting mystery of the blind child that Sadie was supposed to have kept at her home and tended with loving care for many years, but which none of the old timers have identified as hers.

In a rather distorted way, Sadie Orchard certainly achieved her goal. Historically, she has become Hillsboro's first lady and leading citizen. Hillsboro and Sadie are *always* mentioned in the same breath!

## Endnotes:

[1] Clay W. Vaden, "Sadie Orchard, One of New Mexico's Women Stage Drivers," unpublished MS. August 10, 1938, New Mexico Writer's Project File, Library, Museum of New Mexico, Santa Fe. In this interview Sadie stated that she had come to Kingston in 1886. In another personal interview done seventeen months earlier, Sadie stated that she had not arrived until 1888, coming only to operate their newly purchased Kingston stagecoach line while her husband remained in Silver City to run another stage line they also owned. (See Betty Reich, "Stagecoach Days," unpublished MS. March 26, 1937, W.P.A. City File, Museum of New Mexico, Santa Fe.) These frustrating discrepancies apparently occurred as Sadie tried to "re-write" history, pretending she had no earlier career in the "frail sisterhood of fallen women."

[2] Erna Fergusson, *New Mexico: A Pageant of Three Peoples* (New York: Alfred A. Knopf, 1951), p. 294.

[3] Bill Rakocy, *Ghosts of Kingston, Hillsboro, New Mexico* (El Paso, Texas: Bravo Press, 1983), p. 178.

[4] Sadie, speaking about her stage coach line in the 1936 interview with Clay Vaden, said, "Many times I had for passengers some very famous people. Lillian Russell, the stage star, as far as I know was never in Kingston, but members of her troupe were, and I had occasion to meet the actress. She was a guest at one time on a ranch west of Hillsboro, The Horseshoe Ranch, I believe."

[5] Fergusson, p. 294.

[6] Rakocy, p. 50.

[7] William A. Keleher, *The Fabulous Frontier* (Albuquerque: University of New Mexico Press, 1962), p. 264.

[8] *El Paso Times*, November 6, 1938.

[9] Fergusson, p. 308.

[10] Paige W. Christiansen, *The Story of Mining in New Mexico* (Socorro: New Mexico Bureau of Mines & Mineral Resources, 1974), pp. 78-79.

[11] Keleher, p. 264. Keleher presents a very detailed and interesting account of the trial.

[12] William A. Wallace, "Short-Line Staging in Territorial New Mexico," *New Mexico Historical Review* (#2 April 1957): p. 208.

[13] Fergusson, p. 294.

[14] *El Paso Journal*, July 19, 1978.

[15] Today Hot Springs is Truth or Consequences, New Mexico, a name acquired from the television show. For all her love of the gaudy and high-style, Sadie Orchard wound up in a dusty, unkempt cemetery with a simple 18" by 26" gray stone listing only her name and the years 1865-1943, to mark her grave.

[16] Rakocy, p. 22. The author cites former Hillsboro resident, Pete Kenney, as a source of the story that Sadie, on a dare, rode through town "nude as a jaybird," Lady Godiva Style.

# With Unflinching Devotion to Duty

He was an unlikely hero, at least for the times in which he lived. He was a Black soldier in an era when fearsome prejudice and overt, cruel discrimination were the order of the day, in and out of the military. He was probably born a slave, but through his actions became one of the elite company who received a grateful nation's highest military commendation—the Medal of Honor.

First Sergeant Moses Williams began life in 1845 in Carroll Parish (County), Louisiana, a county which no longer exists. In a way, that fact seems rather appropriate, for very few records of Williams' life or career were ever kept—a symbol of the nineteenth century viewpoint that a Black man's life was predestined to be insignificant.

During the Civil War nearly 180,000 Black troops served in the Union Army and by its close 33,380 had given their lives in that great conflict. On July 28, 1866, Congress authorized the creation of six regiments of Black troops for the peacetime army, four of infantry and two of cavalry. The motivation was an attempt to the raise the status of former slaves by giving them career opportunities.

Depiction of a Buffalo Soldier by Frederic Remington.

Nine weeks later, Moses Williams enlisted in the Ninth Cavalry, which was organized in New Orleans. It was a natural decision for a Black man who barely had survived, scratching out a livelihood by farming in the war-ravaged region. The military offered privates a regular and dependable salary of thirteen dollars a month and also a chance for some education, along with an opportunity to make something of one's life and perhaps gain a little dignity from the wearing of a uniform.

Private Moses Williams had found his niche in life. Illiterate when he enlisted, he took advantage of an Army program by which chaplains in the Black regiments taught the soldiers the basics of reading, writing, and math. When he joined the military, Williams signed his enlistment papers with an "X." Five years later when he re-enlisted, Moses Williams proudly wrote his name.[1]

But a military career, while undoubtedly better than his former condition, did not automatically endow Moses Williams with a life of equality, or of respect for his attributes and abilities. As a member of the famed Buffalo Soldiers (reputedly so named by their Plains Indians adversaries who were intrigued by the cavalrymen's short, curly black hair, which they compared to the 'wool' which sprouted between a buffalo's eyes), he and his comrades suffered many injustices throughout the years they served in the West.

Black soldiers had to overcome the prejudice which said they would all be lazy, undisciplined, lacking in initiative, cowardly, and incapable of doing routine work. In actuality, over the decades of their service, these troops proved to be just the opposite. They were brave, loyal, and dependable soldiers, who had a lower desertion rate than the white troops and were considerably less impaired by alcoholism, a common peacetime army affliction. One officer of the Tenth Cavalry said, "By simple mathematical calculation on the cost of deserters...it would appear that in the twenty-three years since the reorganization of the Army, the Government would have saved ten million dollars on the item of desertions alone" if it had been composed entirely of "colored troops."[2]

But in spite of the Black troopers' outstanding records, many white officers refused to lead them. Their units were frequently assigned to the least desirable posts, or even told to camp outside forts manned by white troops. They were commonly assigned broken down and inferior mounts cast off by other units, and were sometimes cheated, robbed, and even killed by the civilians they were sworn to protect.[3] To make matters worse, in some combat situations, their role was ignored or distorted and other soldiers, less deserving, received the praise and credit.

Regarding one campaign against the Cheyennes in 1867 and 1868, an officer said, "The colored men did all the fighting, sustained nearly all the casualties, and the white troops received the commendations."[4]

After completing his initial training, Private Williams, along with other members of the Ninth Cavalry, moved west in the summer of 1867. Their initial orders were to man Forts Davis and Stockton in Texas to protect the mail and stage route between San Antonio and El Paso. Their foes were the marauding tribes which swarmed over the areas—the Mescalero Apaches from New Mexico, and the Kiowa and Comanche warriors from the north, who spread terror all the way south, even into Mexico.

In addition to the hostile Indians, Williams and his fellow horse soldiers faced other hardships. Mexican bandits and revolutionaries ignored the national boundaries and operated where they pleased. *Comancheros* plied their illegal trade in whisky, guns, and ammunition for stolen livestock, and the area was a wide-open playground for all types of armed and unethical adventurers and Civil War veterans unable to settle back into a law-abiding lifestyle.

Compounding these problems was a populace of Texans, chagrined by defeat and struggling with Reconstruction, which had little tolerance for Union soldiers, much less Blacks. In addition, the lack of sufficient military manpower to cover the vast frontier and the need to completely rebuild the forts where the men were stationed, put an added burden on the cavalrymen.

# Unflinching Devotion

Moses Williams was posted to Fort Davis, in Presidio County, in West Texas. From there the troopers spent many weary hours in the saddle scouting for the hostiles, guarding both wagon trains and mail carriers across the barren stretches of wilderness, chasing stolen stock, and actually learning, through on-the-job training one might say, the tricks and foibles of their Indian adversaries.

In addition to their duties in the field, the troopers found themselves working as laborers, carpenters, masons, and even farmers, as they toiled cutting logs, digging ditches, planting gardens, erecting adobe buildings, and reconstructing the post, almost from the ground up.

Moses Williams, apparently, found Army life not unpleasant, even though the Buffalo Soldiers literally "rode their mounts into the ground," through debilitating heat or bitter cold, as they covered vast expanses in their pursuit of Indians.

His regiment was ably commanded by Colonel Edward Hatch, a white officer who, after receiving citations for gallantry and meritorious service, had closed out the Civil War as brevet major general of the volunteers. Colonel Hatch was not only a decisive and competent leader whose good judgment enabled him to get the most from his troops, but also a personable man who led the regiment for many years, and whose loyalty to his troopers was unflagging.[5]

During the early months of 1870, Williams' troop, "I," was sent on several scouts northwestward into Mescalero country, where they chased and fought the Indians in the rugged, almost inaccessible regions of the Guadalupe Mountains. Before one fifty-three day scout was over, the men were in wretched condition, their boots in pieces, their clothes in tatters, and half the command dismounted because so many horses had been lost.

After the scout an officer wrote that the troops had "...marched about 1,000 miles, over two hundred of which was through country never explored by troops...drove the Indians from every *rancheria*...destroyed immense amounts of food, robes, skins, utensils...captured forty horses and mules."

## From Martyrs to Murderers

Colonel Edward Hatch was an able and much respected commander of the Ninth Cavalry.
(Author's Collection)

He also described the Black troops as "peculiarly adapted to hunting Indians," saying they were "always cheerful and ready to brave the severest hardships without a murmur despite short rations and, often, no water."[6]

Such was the life Trooper Williams lived. He seemed to thrive on it, learning new skills, serving in a conscientious manner, and advancing through the ranks. For eight long years Williams and the rest of the Ninth Cavalry remained in Texas, garrisoning some of the worst posts on the wild frontier and, in what seemed almost perpetual motion, trying to bring some sort of control and order to the area. Finally, in late 1875, Colonel Hatch received orders to transfer his command to the Department of New Mexico.

By June, 1876, Moses Williams' company was stationed at Fort Wingate, in Navajo country in northwestern New Mexico.[7] The fort was in an isolated area and controlled a military reservation of more than one hundred square miles. It was blessed,

*(above)* Troop H, Ninth Cavalry at Fort Wingate, New Mexico, 1899-1900. (Museum of New Mexico) *(below)* Navajo scouts waiting to be paid at Fort Wingate, New Mexico, in 1886. (U.S. Army Signal Corps Collections in the Museum of New Mexico.)

however, with a good spring of water, wood in the hills, grass in the valley, plenty of game in the surrounding countryside, and a healthful climate.

Even though the Navajos were now peacefully resettled on their traditional lands, Apaches in the Southwest were still at war with the white populace which had invaded their homeland. Repeated attempts to corral the nomadic Apaches onto reservations they objected to failed. In late 1877, an irate Victorio, with three hundred Warm Spring and Chiricahua followers, left the San Carlos Reservation and began marauding.

All available troops in New Mexico were sent out against them, including, of course, Moses Williams, who had, through years of reliable service, attained the rank of sergeant. Soon the mountains were swarming with soldiers and their allied Indian scouts. After a month of raids, depredations, feints against their military pursuers, and constant movement, many of the exhausted Apaches gave up. Sergeant Williams watched as one hundred and ninety came into Fort Wingate to surrender. Later the remainder also gave up. By now Sergeant Williams was an old hand in the pursuit of Apaches.

The problems with Victorio and the Apaches were not permanently solved, however. Two years later, in 1879, he and his band escaped from the Mescalero Reservation in southern New Mexico and, once again, rode westward into the wilds. Before they had traveled ten miles, Victorio swooped down upon the horse guard of Company E, Ninth Cavalry, at Ojo Caliente, killing or wounding eight men and capturing forty-six horses. In spite of the cavalrymen's desperate attempts to apprehend the culprits in several bloody skirmishes, the Apaches evaded capture. They ranged through the mountains, subsisting on sheep they murdered Mexican sheepherders to obtain.

Colonel Hatch, resolved to bring the offenders to justice for the deaths of his troopers, mounted a determined campaign. He took personal command of operations in the field, ordered the entire Ninth Cavalry into southern New Mexico, requested and received reinforcements of soldiers and Indian scouts from

Arizona, and even obtained a troop from the Sixth U. S. Cavalry for the great effort. Sergeant Williams and Troop I were transferred from Fort Wingate to the post at Ojo Caliente, situated near the Rio Grande in southwestern New Mexico, right in the area where Victorio and his band had been living.

During the early spring of 1880, Victorio added about one hundred renegades from Old Mexico to his band, and then convinced an additional two hundred Mescalero Apaches to join him, fifty of whom were experienced fighting braves. In spite of the best efforts of the more than one thousand troops in the field against him, Victorio, with approximately two hundred fifty warriors, continued to raid and fill the hearts of area residents with terror.

Finally, by June, almost two thousand cavalrymen and several hundred scouts were in constant pursuit. This pressure forced Victorio to escape into Mexico, where he was safe, because U. S. troops were not permitted to cross the boundary.

During these months of conflict at least two hundred settlers and soldiers were killed in New Mexico, approximately an equal number in Old Mexico, and at least one hundred of the Indians were slain. We can only imagine the disappointment and anger Sergeant Williams and the other exhausted troopers felt when Victorio escaped. However, they must have been considerably cheered four months later when word was received that the indomitable old chief and many of his followers had been killed by Mexican troops at Tres Castillos, Mexico, in October, 1880. Moses Williams, by now a fourteen-year veteran of the Indian Wars, may have thought his Apache-chasing days were over. Little did he know!

After Victorio's death, small bands of Apaches continued their raids and exacted their revenge against the military. In January 1881, Apaches attacked a stage near Fort Cummings and killed the driver and a passenger. Sergeant Williams was most likely with the detachment from Company I which, with several others, unsuccessfully chased the culprits. The Indians fled back and forth across the international boundary, as it suited them, to avoid capture.

## From Martyrs to Murderers

Victorio, Warm Spring Chief

While these small raids continued, Nana, an elderly and embittered Apache who had been one of Victorio's lieutenants, collected a corps of determined warriors and weapons and began a four-month campaign against the whites, which created absolute terror in the hearts of the locals. While the troops, and even parties of civilians chased Nana's band, the Indians, as General Pope later said, "rushed through the country from one mountain range to another like a pack of hungry wolves, killing everybody they met and stealing all the horses they could get their hands on."[8]

On August 16, 1881, Company I was camped near Cuchillo Negro (Black Ridge) Peak, which, ironically, was named after a famous Apache chieftain who had been a contemporary of Geronimo. It was almost noon when a hysterical Mexican-American raced into camp, shouting that the Apaches had attacked his nearby ranch and butchered his family. "Boots and Saddles" was immediately sounded. Lieutenant George Burnett, a white officer, with First Sergeant Williams and fourteen other troopers immediately, saddled up and raced off to the scene of the murders. Another lieutenant, Gustavus Valois, was to round up the rest of the company and follow. When the soldiers arrived they were distressed to find the mutilated bodies of the man's wife and three children.

The marauders' trail was clearly visible and Burnett and his men, reinforced by a few local Hispanos, took up the pursuit. Within a few miles they overtook the Apaches in the foothills of the Cuchillo Negro but, as usual, the Apaches were in effective defensive positions among the rocks and crevices.

Lieutenant Burnett deployed his available manpower in three wings, leading one himself, putting First Sergeant Williams on the right, and placing a local Hispano in charge on the left. After pouring fire into the Apache positions, it became clear to Burnett that they could not be dislodged, so he attempted to flank them with a handful of men. Almost immediately he found himself in dire straits, nearly surrounded. When Trumpeter John Rogers volunteered to go for aid through a hail of bullets, Burnett agreed. Rogers made it safely through and united with the arriving Lieutenant Valois and his detachment, who hurried forward.

The Indians shifted and poured a volley into Company I, killing ten horses. A melee then ensued while Burnett and his men fought their way to Valois. The united command then fell back to a safer position. Unfortunately, in the bedlam, four troopers failed to hear the order to retreat and the Apaches quickly moved to isolate them.

Without a moment's hesitation, Burnett, Williams, and a Private Augustus Walley dashed forward to their rescue. Several of the imperiled men were wounded. Williams and Burnett, with bullets flying all around them, began a covering fire even though they were badly outnumbered and in an extremely exposed position. While they kept up the fusillade, Private Walley pulled the wounded men to safety.

The fighting continued for hours. At one point troops in the rear panicked and started to retreat when Lieutenant Burnett's horse broke free and raced away. They feared he was dead. Williams, exposing himself to dangerous gunfire, raced after the soldiers and brought them back to fight.

The combat continued until nightfall, when Nana disengaged and quietly slipped away in the darkness. His trail headed south. In the days that followed, Company I and other troopers chased Nana's band in an attempt to halt their escape to Mexico. Other Ninth Regiment men would be killed and wounded in the pursuit before the Indians successfully stole away.

Nana's raid was the "last hurrah" for the Ninth Cavalry in the Southwest. They had endured years of rigorous service in New Mexico, Colorado, and Texas. General Pope, appreciating their efforts, awarded them a much deserved rest, ordering them to less demanding posts in Kansas and Oklahoma.

## From Martyrs to Murderers

Sergeant Williams, however, had made his mark on history. He, Lieutenant Burnett, and Private Walley were all recommended for the Medal of Honor for their actions in the fighting at Cuchillo Negro. All three eventually received it. In citing Williams for his Medal, Burnett wrote,

> I...recommend him for a Medal of Honor for his bravery in volunteering to come to my assistance, his skill in conducting the right flank in a running fight of three or four hours, his keen-sightedness in discovering the Indians in hiding and which probably prevented my command from falling into a trap, for the skill and ability displayed by him in rallying my men when I was dismounted and unable to reach them and lastly for his coolness, bravery, and unflinching devotion to duty in standing by me in an open position under a heavy fire from a large party of Indians at a comparatively short range, and thus enabling me to undoubtedly save the lives of at least three other men.[9]

Moses Williams continued to serve as a cavalryman for fifteen years before the Medal was finally awarded to him on November 12, 1896. Two years later, after thirty-two years as a Buffalo Soldier, Moses Williams retired from the Army. He had dedicated a lifetime to the Ninth Cavalry, forsaking such human pleasures as a wife, family, home ownership, and permanent place of residence.

Sadly, only one year later, Moses Williams died in Vancouver, Washington, at the age of fifty-four. His death drew only a terse, five-line notice in the August 25, 1899, local newspaper. It was not until a rival newspaper printed an account of William's bravery and national award that the Vancouver newspaper mentioned his feat, and even then they only reprinted the already-published article.

Even more melancholy is the fact that the official record of William's death, sent to Army headquarters from the commanding officer of the Vancouver Barracks, stated, "the sergeant died alone and without friends."

# Unflinching Devotion

Endnotes:

[1] Sgt. Moses Williams' Military Service Records, National Archives, Washington, D.C.

[2] Bernard C. Nalty, *Strength For the Fight: A History of Black Americans in the Military* (New York: The Free Press, 1986), p. 52.

[3] It is amazing that the Buffalo Soldiers rose above the overt discrimination shown them by both the military and civil authorities. William H. Leckie in his *The Buffalo Soldiers: A Narrative of the Negro Cavalry in the West* (Norman: University of Oklahoma Press, 1967), cites innumerable specific cases of the unfair treatment to which these men were subject. For example, two of Moses Williams' fellow soldiers in Co. I were each sentenced to a dishonorable discharge and one year at hard labor; one for the minor offense of pilfering a jar of candy from a saloon and the other for stealing one dollar from a civilian. Such penalties would never have been imposed on white soldiers. The Black soldiers were provisioned with inferior food; even the post surgeon at Fort Concho cited the lack of staples common at other posts, including potatoes and onions, and the fact that the bread was sour, the butter made of suet, and only enough flour for the white officers was provided.

[4] Nalty, p. 54.

[5] Hatch, a blond, blue-eyed native of Maine was only one of the excellent white officers the Buffalo Soldiers were fortunate enough to serve under. Major Albert P. Morrow would later command the Ninth Cavalry for fifteen years, turning it into a tough, hard-hitting unit renowed for always arriving to the rescue in the nick of time. Another excellent officer was Lt. Col. Wesley Merritt, who proudly described his Black troopers as "brave in battle, easily disciplined, and most efficient in the care of the horses, arms and equipment." General John J. 'Black Jack' Pershing of World War I fame, proudly led the Tenth Cavalry for more than a decade when he was a young lieutenant. George Armstrong Custer was offered a lieutenant colonelcy with the Ninth Cavalry when it was being organized and refused it — probably the luckiest thing that ever happened to Williams and his comrades.

[6] Leckie, pp. 92-93.

[7] S. C. Agnew, *Garrisons of the Regular U.S. Army, New Mexico, 1846-1899* (Santa Fe: Press of the Territorian, 1971), p. 77

[8] *Annual Report of the Secretary of War for the Year 1881*, p. 117.

[9] *Medal of Honor Recipients, 1863-1973*, Congressional Committee Print 15, Committee on Veterans' Affairs, United States Senate, Washington: U.S. Printing Office, 1973), p. 330.

# The Midnight Stranglers

It was dark and quiet in the Socorro, New Mexico Territory, jail that October night in 1881, but the young prisoners, Bush Clark and Frenchy Elmoreau, couldn't sleep. It was not the making of escape plans which kept them awake. Both knew escape was impossible, for each was securely shackled by chains anchored to a huge boulder embedded in the earth of their basement prison. And several lawmen were nearby to guard them.

It was fear that was gnawing at their insides, driving away all chance of rest, keeping them tense and wide-eyed. They were filled with dread that the Socorro Stranglers would be coming after them.

Just at daybreak that Thursday morning, October 6, they had been surprised and captured in town. Several other members of their party had escaped into the nearby mountains, taking with them the money the band had acquired when they robbed the Browne and Manzanares branch commission house, a store at Lamy Junction, just east of Santa Fe, about a week earlier.

# The Midnight Stranglers

The robbery had netted them about a thousand dollars in money and goods. They had taken the one hundred and sixty-five dollars from the cash drawer, along with the pocket money and valuables of the store's proprietor and his three customers. In addition, they had helped themselves to a load of merchandise, including food, pistols and rifles, ammunition, saddles, and other provisions, which they transported in the proprietor's personal wagon, pulled by his own team of horses. Then they had ridden away under the cover of approaching darkness.

After that escapade they rode southward down the Rio Grande Valley. Along the way they had encountered, by pure chance, a lone traveler. Taking advantage of their good fortune, they held him up and relieved him of his horse, one hundred and fifty dollars in currency, and an expensive chronometer.

Continuing down river, the gang had a close call when Sheriff Connolley of Los Lunas spotted them but, unsure of their guilt and having no warrant, he failed to arrest them. The incident, however, scared the robbers, and they laid low for several days. Success made them all a little cocky, though. Since there are certain things red-blooded men can't do without, sooner or later they were going to have to go into a town to get them. Their mistake was in choosing Socorro.

They should have known better. It was well understood up and down the Rio Grande that Socorro, a boom town filled with prospectors, cowboys, gamblers, ranchers, miners, and plenty of saloons and gambling halls, was a place rascals should avoid. As one newspaper put it, "They get out the Stranglers on the least provocation."[1]

Only a year earlier it would have been a lot safer for Frenchy and Bush to have ridden into the vicinity of Socorro and been caught by the Mexican-American sheriff, even though they had been members of Ike Stockton's outlaw gang, which had recently disintegrated after the killing of its leader.

But in December 1880, after the Christmas Eve killing of the town's Anglo newspaper editor by a Spanish-speaking resident, all the non-Hispanic men of Socorro had banded together into a vigilante group to dispense their own harsh form of justice. They called themselves the Socorro Committee of Safety.

## From Martyrs to Murderers

But the town's Mexican-American population called them *Los Colgadores*, or The Hangers. Others called them The Socorro Stranglers.

When the vigilantes first organized, they were open and above board about their intentions. The New Year's Day 1881, issue of the local newspaper even published a list of the entire membership, printing it in both Spanish and English.[2] Accompanying the names was the warning: "Notice is hereby given that all violations of peace and good order by any person or persons, irrespective of nationality and condition, will be meritabley followed by speedy and sure punishment."

Within three months of their organization, the vigilantes proved they were serious about putting 'Judge Lynch' in charge. Tom Gordon, who had killed Socorro's marshal the year before by shooting him in the back through a saloon window, was spotted fleeing Socorro in a railroad freight car. Socorro lawmen followed on the next train and waited until the miscreant disembarked near Albuquerque. Although surrounded by Winchester-toting deputies, Gordon refused to surrender until his captors promised that he would get a fair trial if returned to Socorro.

That very night, however, a large vigilante group described by one witness as "hung all over with shooters," removed Gordon from jail and, even though he resisted furiously, hustled him right through the center of town to a corral gate. Gordon pleaded to be shot instead of hung but a noose was thrown around his neck. The prisoner struggled wildly, and in the uproar Gordon managed to savagely clamp his teeth onto the fingers of one of his tormentors. The vigilante screamed in pain, pulled out his six-shooter with his free hand, and struck Gordon over the head. That action rendered him unconscious and inadvertently made his death easier when he was hoisted heavenward.

After Gordon's hanging, the reign of the rope continued, and several other unfortunates were forced to wear a hemp necktie. No wonder Frenchy and Bush were terrified! When they were thrown into their cell it was with the understanding

## The Midnight Stranglers

Colonel Ethan W. Eaton, rancher, mine owner, former militia officer, and Socorro's leading citizen was the man who organized the "Committee of Safety." (Univ. of New Mexico Library Special Collections)

that they would stay there until officers from Santa Fe County arrived to return them northward to stand trial. This was certainly their hope. After all, they had done nothing as grave as killing a sheriff. Perhaps they would be given sentences to serve in the Santa Fe jail, or, at worst, be sent to the Kansas State Penitentiary where New Mexicans burdened with longer sentences were incarcerated.

But, as the day wore on, they discovered they had been captured by Colonel E. W. Eaton, Socorro's leading citizen and the organizer and leader of the vigilantes! They also learned how, earlier that year, a crowd of hundreds of the town's vigilantes had snatched a prisoner from renowned Texas Ranger James Gillette and hung him. No wonder hope became harder to maintain and dread tightened their guts. No doubt they mentally cursed their ignorance of the vengeful mood of Socorro's citizens, which had caused them to fail to give the town a wide berth while fleeing southward.

## From Martyrs to Murderers

Midnight was the time of preference for the Socorro Stranglers to gather and pluck their victims from the arms of the law. Just as the two youthful lawbreakers had feared, at twelve o'clock a posse of masked men, about one hundred strong, appeared at the jail, leveled their guns at the unsurprised guards, and took the prisoners on their last walk.

The vigilantes escorted the pair to a narrow street just off the main plaza. As they stumbled, terrified, through the darkness, surrounded by the armed and almost jovial mob, they came to a spot where the lane curved. Here they were told to stop. Behind the adobe wall that bordered the roadway grew a large cottonwood tree whose branches reached over the alley. This would be the instrument of their death.

The thoroughfare—known to some as Palisades Alley, and to others as Death Alley—ran behind the livery stable, connected the residential section of town to the main plaza, and was only half a block from the Methodist Church.[3] Someone in the crowd suggested, in jest, that the pastor should witness the lynching. The mob shouted its approval; twenty men were dispatched to the parsonage and the minister was routed out of bed, compelled to dress, and brought to the scene.

Now the crowd was ready. The two men were lifted to the top of the tall adobe wall and nooses placed around their necks. The other ends of the ropes were thrown over the limbs of the giant cottonwood.

Frenchy, at the portals of the unknown, lost his nerve and begged pitifully for his life. Apparently the weaker of the two men, earlier he had confessed both to being a member of the gang and to his crimes while Bush, although younger, had refused to incriminate himself. Bush, disgusted, now cursed Frenchy for his weakness and when the order came to "shove them off," Bush's last words to the crowd were, "I'll meet you _____s all in hell."[4]

The following day a local reporter wrote that "...the citizens of this quiet city were surprised this morning in finding the stiffs of Clark and Frenchy...hanging chained together...with a placard on their backs saying, 'This is the way Socorro treats horse thieves and footpads.' This seems to be an unhealthy part of New Mexico for bad men. It is said they died game."[5]

Another reporter, with a macabre sense of humor, sent the following dispatch to the Santa Fe newspapers:

> The two Lamy thieves who were arrested Wednesday were found dangling from a cottonwood tree this morning. It is situated just at the turn of the lane and it is supposed the twain were perambulating this narrow lane and ran against the curve and, desiring to make a straight cut, attempted to jump the fence, and in doing so jumped into a noose rope that was dangling from this tree. But the fact of there being two nooses tied after the fashion of a hangman's knot at the end of each rope which passes over the limb on the opposite side near the ground, makes the accident somewhat obscure. There is another coincident [sic] that looks strange, in the way of a placard upon the back of Bush. It reads: The fate of footpads and horse thieves. Then there is a piece of jewelry attached to the twain that is a good imitation of a pair of shackles that securely fastens one leg of each to the other. How the mischief they expected to get over this fence by such a device looks strange in light of the fact that Frenchy was taller than Bush and it can readily be seen that Frenchy must jump higher than Bush, and consequently, Bush must have felt the solidity of the rope over the limb before Frenchy. That must be the case as Bush was found staring into the heavens in search of the other end of the rope while Frenchy was looking down to see how much he was raised above the fence; but the whole thing was a useless waste of strength, as they failed to come down, and were found hanging to that little limb this morning.
> 
> Frenchy Elmoreau was a rather tall man, with dark hair...about twenty-eight years of age and upon his countenance there was an expression that showed that his last thoughts must have been of the bad acts of his life. Bush Clark (that being the only name he would give), was of medium stature, with blond hair and countenance, and about twenty-one years of age. His mug was an ugly one and looked as though he was mad.[6]

# From Martyrs to Murderers

Frenchy Elmoreau and Bush Clark were hung from a cottonwood tree by the Socorro vigilantes in October 1881. One of the men's hats can be seen perched on the rough adobe wall beneath their feet, along with the handmade sign pinned to one of the dead men's coat. (Author's Collection)

# The Midnight Stranglers

The two men's bodies were the subject of much curiosity, and early in the morning a crowd gathered in the lane to view them. They were then cut down and taken to the nearby livery stable, where a jury was assembled about 9 a.m. It soon arrived at the verdict that the two men had come to their deaths by strangulation, caused by a rope tied around their necks by "unknown parties."

Of course, every person in town was well aware of the identities of the vigilantes, particularly since almost all Anglo males above the age of eighteen had been coerced into becoming members.

The only personal property found on the outlaws' bodies consisted of a one cent piece, a beer check, some tobacco, and a match safe. At the time they were captured, the culprits also had three horses, five revolvers, a Navajo blanket and one rifle. One of the horses was identified as taken during the Brown and Manzanares Company robbery, but the stolen money was never recovered. It was assumed to have been carried by Bush Clark's brother, who got away.

For all practical purposes, the Socorro vigilantes became an outlaw organization. They punished perceived lawbreakers in various ways. Some were given from twenty to one hundred lashes on their bare backs with a great whip wielded by the town blacksmith, a large and powerful man. Others were run out of town, or escorted to the railroad and told to "count the ties."

There was no recourse against judgments made by the Socorro Committee of Safety. Not only were all the leading businessmen members, but also all the town's doctors, the judge, the bankers, attorneys, saloon proprietors, and even the three ministers. In fact, membership was apparently obligatory among the Anglo male population. Any member in town was forced to attend meetings which were preliminary to lynchings.

Once the town's banker failed to show up and a committee of ten men was sent to his home. When the man's wife informed the visitors that he was already in bed and did not wish to be

(*above*) When gold and silver were discovered in the mountains near Socorro, the town boomed, filling with prospectors, cowboys, miners, gamblers, and "soiled doves." (*below*) Dark deeds may have taken place at night in Socorro but, by day, one might see a large procession of Hispanic Catholics celebrating a feast day. Socorro's Hispanics were neither recruited nor welcomed to membership in the vigilantes. (Author's Collection)

disturbed, someone quietly remarked, "Get a rope."[7] In an instant the banker was on the front porch in his night clothes, requesting time to dress.

The discovery of gold and silver in the nearby mountains had brought a great influx of outsiders to Socorro. One gambling emporium, run by a man who used ten dollar gold pieces set with diamonds as coat and cuff buttons, kept a staff of faro dealers who worked eight-hour shifts so that uninterrupted play could continue twenty-four hours a day. The dance halls were ablaze at night and women with names such as 'Rocky-faced Kate,' and 'Hop Fiend Kit,' danced and drank on commission. This environment provided plenty of opportunities for the vigilantes to find lawbreakers they felt needed their attention.

At least three more men would be hung by the Socorro Committee of Safety before it disbanded in 1884. After Charley Russell was elected sheriff, everyone agreed that he would be able to keep the town safe.

Frenchy Elmoreau and Bush Clark, however, would have the dubious distinction of being remembered in New Mexico history as the objects of the only double hanging carried out by the Socorro Stranglers.

Endnotes:

[1] *The Daily Optic*, Las Vegas, New Mexico, October 7, 1881.
[2] Chester D. Potter, "Reminiscences of the Socorro Vigilantes," Paige W. Christiansen, ed., *New Mexico Historical Review* 40, No. 1 (January 1965): 29.
[3] Ibid., p. 35; *Santa Fe Daily New Mexican*, October 8, 1881.
[4] *New Mexico Historical Review* 40, p. 35.
[5] *Santa Fe Daily New Mexican*, October 8, 1881.
[6] Ibid. The two men were reputed to be members of Ike Stockton's gang, which had earlier terrorized parts of Colorado. In various accounts, Clark is referred to as Jim Bush, 'The Kid,' and 'Butch.'
[7] *New Mexico Historical Review* 40, pp. 34-35.

# A Bitter Price

The 1850s—it was a terrible time to be living in northern Mexico. The Apaches were raiding southward from across the United States border at will; they had penetrated as far south as Mazatlan and devastated it. In Sonora, hundreds of citizens were slaughtered and thousands of animals stolen each year. In fact, the Apaches of the Gila considered Sonora as a convenient "*rancho* and supply depot."[1]

So, for the marauding band of Apaches on a raid deep into Mexico, it seemed nothing more than a routine incident when they snatched and kidnapped the young boy. Little did they know, as they carried off the squalling, terrified child, that in the years to come their tribe would pay a bitter price for their actions.

It was 1853 when Merejildo Grijalva was plucked from the bosom of his family and home in a tiny Sonora town about one hundred miles south of the border.[2] There was nothing unusual about the event; every year hundreds of children were stolen by the Indians. Most were quickly and successfully indoctrinated into their nomadic way of life.

Grijalva's captors were Arizona Apaches, members of Narbona's band, which, within a few years, came under the control of Cochise. They forced him to remain with them in the years that followed, even requiring him to accompany them during their frequent raids back into Mexico to steal livestock. As a bright boy, Grijalva easily learned the Apache ways. But, as a stubborn boy, he refused to forget his origins. As he grew older, he watched for an opportunity to escape.

After approximately ten years of captivity, the now-grown Grijalva fled from his captors. Why he left after so many years is a matter for speculation. Two explanations have been put forth. The first is that he learned of the death of five of his brothers at the hands of the tribe. The other, and more romantic, is that he fell in love with an Apache girl, took her as his wife, and she was then abducted and killed by some irresponsible warriors.[3] The truth may be less glamorous. Captives were not highly esteemed and often harshly dealt with or killed, and Grijalva probably was tired of being used as a servant. With the help of the station keeper at Apache Pass, Arizona, who gave him sanctuary, he regained his freedom. He then made his way to Fort Thorn on the Rio Grande in south-central New Mexico, and found employment with Dr. Michael Steck, who served as agent for the Southern Apaches.

Later, Grijalva acquired a job as a guide, scout, and interpreter for the military garrison at Fort Bowie, Arizona. At the time, a large campaign was being waged against the Arizona Apaches by General James Carleton, military commander of the Territory, who earlier had successfully subdued the Navajos and forced them onto a reservation in eastern New Mexico.

On July 10, 1864, a scouting party of fifty-seven California and New Mexico Volunteer soldiers left Bowie to search for Apaches in the ravine-filled western slopes of the Chiricahua Mountains.[4] Merejildo Grijalva was their guide. The party would be gone for twenty-three days, march more than three hundred miles, and range as far as the Mexican border.

From the onset the scouting party was plagued by bad weather. On July 15, while the unit was camped in a heavy downpour, guards discovered several Indians climbing up a steep mountain about a mile from camp.[5] Grijalva, with twenty-one soldiers, was dispatched in pursuit. As they climbed the rugged slopes in the driving rain, toward the area where the Apaches had been seen, they were hailed, in Spanish, by a brave standing on an almost perpendicular cliff about one hundred feet above them.

The Indian shouted that he was a warrior and a brave one and commenced shooting arrows. When the arrows failed to inflict any damage on the soldiers he began to throw rocks, severely bruising the arms of one of the California volunteers. The troops, meanwhile, fired at him and he soon fell. Mortally wounded, he called out for Grijalva, whom he had recognized.

Grijalva's intimate knowledge of the Apaches and their ways made him extremely cautious. He would not approach the downed man until he was satisfied that the warrior could no longer use his bow and arrows. He tried to elicit information from the brave about other Indians in the area but the man refused to divulge anything and soon died. Grijalva identified him as an Apache chief named Old Plume. The scout reported that the dead Indian was guilty of numerous murders and robberies, was sullen and tyrannical among his own people, and merciless to all others.

Captain Thomas Tidball, the Army officer in charge of the scouting party, lacking the intimate knowledge of Apaches which Grijalva had acquired so painfully, took a more romantic view of Old Plume. He speculated that the chief could easily have made his escape, and had either halted to cover the retreat of the women and children with him, or else had considered it unworthy of a brave chief to run. The officer believed, in either case, it was an act of heroism worthy of admiration.

The following day, after marching only four miles, the troops heard Indians "hallooing" from the cliffs. Captain Tidball sent Grijalva to talk to the Apaches, to tell them to come into camp to make a treaty. While the troops waited, Grijalva and the Indians parlayed "long distance" for four hours. Finally, four braves descended as far as a grove of trees a mile from the

# Bitter Price

troops. One Apache finally came forward, but not too close, and said that some of their group belonged to Mangas Colorado's band, and others were with Cochise. He promised they would come into Fort Bowie within eight days with their people to make a treaty but, in reality, the Apaches were only toying with the soldiers. Frequently, during the expedition, Apache signal fires were seen on the cliffs—fires which indicated the direction of the troop's movement to other Indians up ahead.

Over the next few days an almost humorous cat-and-mouse game took place. Using various tactics, secret ploys, and strategies of misdirection, the Army officer tried to distract the Apaches' attention in order to sneak up on them, but nothing was successful. By July 21, the Apaches openly taunted the troops, and two braves boldly followed them on horseback.

Once again, the now-totally frustrated captain sent Grijalva out to talk to them. The braves refused to allow him near until he returned to camp and left his musket, probably an unnecessary demand since Grijalva was, in fact, an indifferent marksman. Finally one of the Apaches, Ka-eet-sah, an old acquaintance of Grijalva's, came down to talk, leaving the other brave further back to act as a lookout.

Ka-eet-sah deceitfully swore there were no Apaches in the Chiricahuas except for two small bands. Then, with feigned innocence, he asked why the troops had returned to an old camp, thereby slyly demonstrating that he and his band had not been fooled by the Army captain's decoy tactics.

With equal guile, Grijalva replied that the purpose had been to send word to Fort Bowie that the Apaches were coming in within eight days as they had promised and that they were to be received kindly.

The game of wits continued for a short time, with the two men trading lies and banter. Finally the Apache agreed to come into the soldier's camp to speak to the officer, but he told Grijalva that he wanted to smoke first.

The pleased guide gave Ka-eet-sah some of his own tobacco and walked back to camp to report his success. The Apache leisurely enjoyed his smoke, then suddenly jumped onto his horse and rode off rapidly. The outwitted Grijalva was furious with Captain Tidball because he hadn't shot the duplicitous Indian.

At the close of the scout Captain Tidball wrote his report to headquarters. In it he acknowledged that Grijalva was thoroughly acquainted with the Chiricahua Mountains and the habits of the Apaches, but stated that the guide was "constitutionally timid, knowing as he did, the terrible fate awaiting him if he were ever captured." He said that Grijalva would not venture out of sight of the soldiers. "If he was compelled to go he allowed his fears to overcome his judgment and his regard for the truth."[6]

However, other officers evaluated Grijalva's character more charitably, citing his abilities as an excellent tracker, knowledgeable guide, and responsible leader of scouting parties. One wrote, "...he also had a wholesome fear of falling into the hands of the Apaches alive," citing Grijalva's awareness that the Indians would recognize him, consider him a turncoat, and reserve their most exquisite tortures for him. The officer continued, "Of course, if he could prevent it, he would never be taken alive by them, and he strictly adhered to the right rule observed by everyone in those days to always keep one bullet in reserve."[7]

Merejildo Grijalva's luck continued to hold; he was not put in the position of having to choose between suicide or capture, and he continued to make the Apaches's lives miserable. After the California and New Mexico Volunteers were replaced by Regular Army units in 1866, he continued to perform the same duties for them. When soldiers were sent to the area of the upper San Pedro River to establish a new post, Camp Wallen, Grijalva accompanied them. In short order he built himself a cozy little adobe house nearby, moved his wife in, and enjoyed all the marital comforts while the troopers were living under canvas.

One day a United States mail rider was brought into camp lying in the back of a wagon. Four days earlier he had been waylaid by Apaches in an arroyo near the Patagonia mines.

## Bitter Price

They shot him, shattering his kneecap. The Army surgeon had no choice but to amputate his leg.

Because of the great amount of time which had passed since the incident, the commanding officer had doubts that any scout would be able to find the culprits. Grijalva, however, expressed confidence that his familiarity with Apache thought and habit would allow him to lead the soldiers to them. A party of twenty-five men was then organized and set out to find and follow the Indians's tracks. After some phenomenal tracking, Grijalva led the troops to the Chiricahua Mountains, where he knew the Apaches maintained a *rancheria* and rendezvous point.

On the morning of the sixth day the soldiers suddenly came upon a squaw getting water in the mouth of a hidden canyon. When she spotted the troops she raised a loud alarm and the twenty-five Apaches in the nearby camp ran out of their wickiups and scampered up the steep rocky canyon walls like

An Apache *rancheria* much like those Merejildo Grijalva searched out as a military scout. (Author's Collection)

mountain goats. The soldiers quickly dismounted and began to follow, but it was an uneven contest.

The Apaches, even the women carrying children upon their backs, leaped from boulder to boulder among the spiny cactus and sharp-edged lava rocks. They stopped from time to time to taunt and insult the more awkward soldiers who were laboriously climbing upward. Shouting in Spanish, the Apaches used a vocabulary of the most profane and obscene words imaginable, interspersing them with gestures of the most obvious and indecent description. The Indians paid particular attention to Grijalva, for many recognized him from earlier days when he had lived with them. They not only vilified him, but they let him know in no uncertain terms exactly what terrible punishments they would inflict if they ever laid hands on him.

As the first of the Apaches reached the top and disappeared over the brow of the hill, Grijalva, by now suspicious, urged the lieutenant in charge to order his men to discontinue the chase and return to the canyon floor where the mounts had been left in the care of several troopers.

It was excellent advice. The men descended just in time to ward off a number of clever Apaches who, once they were out of sight, had rapidly climbed down the other side of the ridge and circled back toward the horses in an attempt to stampede them. Although Grijalva's expertise had not resulted in the capture of any enemy on this occasion, the soldiers were able to destroy the *rancheria* and all its stores of food, blankets, and weapons.

On another occasion, about a year later, Grijalva again utilized the knowledge he had gained during his youthful kidnapping and forced imprisonment to thwart his former captors. A wounded Mexican trader staggered into Camp Wallen in November, 1867, to report that his party had been attacked by Apaches in Huachuca Pass.

Immediately "Boots and Saddles" was sounded and thirty soldiers, with Grijalva as guide, left for the site of the massacre. There they found the terribly mutilated bodies of the other three traders. Nearby, Grijalva easily found tracks which showed that eight or nine Apaches had left, heading south, driving stolen cattle before them.[8]

For the next four days, over hills and through rocky, steep-sided canyons, Grijalva tracked the Indians, pushing the military party forward, allowing no cooking fires, little rest, and no noise. As the Apaches entered the rocky foothills of the Chiricahua Mountains, they split into two groups, forcing the guide to choose one set of tracks to pursue. After dark fell, the soldiers spent a miserable, chilly night soaked by torrents of rain which washed out every vestige of Indian tracks.

In the morning, however, Grijalva confidently struck out for a particular canyon, aware that in earlier times Cochise's bands had frequently rendezvoused there after a marauding expedition.

After hours of patient, almost silent maneuvering, the soldiers were able to surprise three Apaches. Two of the braves were chased by soldiers on horseback and cut down by gunfire after they had run quite a distance up the mountain. The third warrior, whose thighbone had been fractured by a soldier's bullet in the original fuselage, crawled into a large fissure in the ground and began shooting arrows at some dismounted troopers who were firing at him.

Grijalva, returning from helping hunt down the other two warriors, approached the Indian's hiding place from the rear. He signaled the soldiers to discontinue their fire, crawled to the edge of the hole, thrust his revolver in and dispatched the Apache with a shot to the head.

Later, unobserved by any of the military men, Grijalva sneaked away and scalped the three dead braves in order to show the hair to a civilian hay contractor who lived in the area. The man had promised him an award of one hundred dollars for each Indian he eliminated.

This grim picture of Merejildo Grijalva, however, is one-sided. Except where hostile Apaches were concerned, the man was warm, friendly, and had a robust sense of humor. One of the funniest practical jokes he played took place while he was working at Camp Wallen.

(*left*) Merejildo Grijalva (Univ. of Arizona Library, Special Collections)

(*below*) This group of peaceful Apaches posed for a photograph during an 1876 visit to Washington, D.C. Merejildo Grijalva is standing in the back row, center. (National Archives)

# Bitter Price

Grijalva became good friends with several of the Army officers, communicating with them in his broken English. One young lieutenant, totally smitten by the exceptional beauty of the daughter of a poor but honorable Mexican family living nearby, approached Grijalva with a request for assistance.[9]

For some time he had been trying, unsuccessfully, to learn Spanish in order to impress the girl. Now he decided it would be very romantic if he and a friend could learn a simple love song in Spanish; one they could sing to the *señorita* while he accompanied himself on his violin. He knew Grijalva sang quite well and wanted to know if the guide could teach the two soldiers the words to a brief song phonetically so they could surprise the young lady by serenading her in her own language.

The lieutenant was overjoyed to find that no persuasion was necessary. When the plan was explained to Grijalva, he enthusiastically agreed to help. Thereafter, for four consecutive days, the troubadours practiced in two-hour sessions. Over and over again they repeated the foreign lyrics of the tune which Grijalva assured them was a love song of deep sentiment; one which would create a great sensation when sung for the Mendoza family and particularly their young daughter.

The following Sunday, adorned in their parade uniforms and groomed to perfection, the suitor and his friend, accompanied by the violin, made a social call upon the girl's family. First the proper amenities had to be observed. Then the young Mendoza daughter, she of the lovely dark eyes and dewy complexion, entertained with a song or two. In due time, with these and other matters out of the way, the lieutenant uncased his violin, tuned up, and began playing the music.

The two vocalists soulfully crooned the melodious words, trying greatly to express the love and passion appropriate to a song of the heart. By the end of the first few lines the lieutenant's friend observed an incongruent look of alarm on the young lady's face and one of increasing anger on that of her grandmother. Unsure what the problem might be, he—nevertheless—tried to catch his companion's eye, but the ardent officer, busy watching his uncertain fingering of the strings, missed the telltale signs and continued to play and sing.

## From Martyrs to Murderers

By the time the men had begun the third line of the ballad, the distraught young lady had covered her blushing face with her shawl. The other members of her indignant family were preparing to do great bodily harm to the two uncouth louts who were warbling such a distasteful ditty.

As the girl's father approached, ax in hand, the two young officers bolted for the door and hared away down the hill, followed by the thrown ax, a firebrand, and the violin case. Not far away, behind a large boulder, they found Grijalva, so overcome with glee at the outcome of his wonderful joke that he could no longer stand and was rolling about on the ground in uncontrollable laughter. It was only after a severe drubbing by the two incensed soldiers that he agreed to visit the irate family, explain the whole matter, and make things right once more.

Merejildo Grijalva continued to work for the government for years, was one of Indian Agent John Clum's most valued assistants, and acted as a guide for General George Crook during his campaign against the Apaches. In 1880, after twenty years of hazardous service, he decided to retire and become a farmer and stockman, "away from the maddening crowd."[10]

But the thrill of danger, the challenge, and the excitement of his previous life were the food of Grijalva's existence and without them he was soon bored. On occasion, he was driven to create his own turmoil and thrills and in the ensuing years he was fined for "firing his gun and breaking windows with rocks" in one town, for drawing his pistol and "shooting up the streets" of another, and, at a third place, of trying to shoot a precinct constable.[11]

Eventually he returned to work at the San Carlos Indian agency as an interpreter, using his skills in Athapascan, Spanish, and English but when old age finally slowed him he returned to his ranch. It was there that he died in 1916, at the age of seventy-five.

Over the years Merejildo Grijalva had more than evened the score for his early kidnapping. He had not only made an excellent livelihood using the skills he had been forced to learn by his captors, but he had also earned a place in Arizona history.

# Bitter Price

Throughout it all the caution he had once been criticized for kept him alive in a very dangerous career. As he once explained, "When you go out hunting for Apaches you have in your mind's eye what you are going to do, but you can never know what you may be led into or what you are going to find. It is a very uncertain business."

## Endnotes:

[1] Frank C. Lockwood, The Apache Indians (1938; reprint. Lincoln and London: University of Nebraska Press, 1987), p. 39.

[2] Some sources state that Grijalva was probably captured several years earlier, around 1850; he apparently was never sure himself. Grijalva's first name is spelled both Merejildo and Merehildo in various documents. The problem arises from the fact that the Spanish "j" is pronounced like "h" in English.

[3] Rita Rush, "'El Chivero'—Merejildo Grijalva," Arizoniana, Vol. 1, No. 1, Spring 1960, p. 8.

[4] Company returns, Co. A, New Mexico Infantry Vols., July, 1864, Record Group 94, Compiled Service Records of Volunteer Union Soldiers Who Served in Organizations From the Territory of New Mexico, National Archives, Washington, D.C.

[5] Excerpts from Captain T. T. Tidball's report of the scout appeared in the Santa Fe WeeklyGazette, October 15, 1864, and revealed many details of the hardships the party experienced. Tidball refers to Grijalva by the name "Berriguildi" throughout, apparently a corruption of Merejildo.

[6] Ibid.

[7] A. M. Gustafson, ed., John Spring's Arizona (Tucson: University of Arizona Press, 1966), p. 99.

[8] Ibid., pp. 121-25.

[9] Ibid., pp. 70-73.

[10] Charles D. Poston, "An Historical Veteran," Arizona Enterprise, February 7, 1891.

[11] Rush, pp. 8-10.

# Swept Away By the Deluge

Only the crickets' chirping broke the quiet of the hot, still night in the small town of Folsom, New Mexico Territory, on August 27, 1908. Some miles to the northwest, up on Johnson Mesa, lightning flashed and rain fell, but most of Folsom's five hundred or more residents, in bed and asleep, were unaware of the storm.

It was about 11:00 p.m. when the telephone switchboard's night alarm began to ring insistently in Sarah J. Rooke's small cottage near the north end of town. Sarah ran a small gift shop during the day and manned Folsom's telephone exchange at night.

Sarah awoke instantly, aware that a call at this hour would not be routine. But it took a few moments to sit up, slide her feet into slippers, and make her way to the operator's chair, for she was sixty-eight years old and crippled. When she plugged into her small switchboard she heard the excited voice of a subscriber who lived on a ranch in the uplands. The caller warned Mrs. Rooke that a cloudburst had occurred on Johnson Mesa, resulting in floodwaters which were plunging down toward the town.

# Swept Away

"It's raining so hard up here the wash tubs are running over with water! You better get out before you're swept away!"[1]

Sarah Rooke immediately recognized the danger. Folsom, a thriving cattle-shipping center in the northeast corner of New Mexico, was situated in a narrow canyon. The town was bisected by a normally dry arroyo known as the Dry Cimarron River. A short distance above Folsom two stream beds converged. If each carried water from a downpour on the immense watershed in the mountains above, the resulting flash flood could be devastating.

There was not much time, perhaps one half hour or a little more, before the deluge hit. Sarah Rooke had a decision to make. She was aware that with each call she completed she would be able to warn a whole family of the impending disaster. She was only one woman, and an old one at that. She deliberately decided to remain at her post.

With trembling fingers she plugged into the first customer's jack, cranked the magneto, waited for the ring to be answered, and then offered a brief warning,

"Pack up and leave at once. A flood is coming down the valley."[2]

Time after time she rang subscribers as rapidly as she could, waiting impatiently for sleepy residents to rouse themselves and come to the phone to receive the warning from central, aware that every precious wasted moment was vital. The great churning wall of water, picking up debris and speed as it rushed on, was rapidly coming closer.

Sarah Rooke, known affectionately to the townspeople as Sally, had managed to reach more than forty families before the thunder of the approaching deluge was heard. A few failed to heed her warning and paid with their lives. But most were able to flee to safety on higher ground before the great inundation, funneled through the narrow canyon, hit the town with terrible force. Those who did not have telephones or did not flee were swept away to their deaths.

Sarah's cottage was one of the first to be hit by the great wall of water and swallowed up. The murderous torrent tore

(*left*) Sarah J. (Sally) Rooke, 68-year-old telephone operator, who saved many lives during the Folsom flood. (Author's Collection)

(*below*) After the flood water receded, the remains of the little telephone office, which had been attached to Sarah Rooke's home, were found smashed against a larger building which had withstood the watery onslaught.
(Raymond Morrow Ranch, Jane Morrow Owensby)

loose everything in its path. It was a nightmare of terror, helplessness, and chaos. One horrified observer who had climbed to safety saw a neighbor's house floating down the stream with the occupants, in their nightclothes, madly running from room to room with lamps in their hands, screaming for help. A strong man, he almost fainted at the sight and cursed his inability to aid them as the bobbing home disappeared when the wild current swept it away.[3] The inhabitants, the town's leading merchant and his family, eventually perished when the home was dashed to pieces at Cimarron Falls, eight miles further down the canyon.

The great wall of water was reported to have been thirteen feet high and a mile wide.[4] Practically the entire business district and a great portion of the residential section was washed down the stream. One reporter wrote that any surviving business houses had been flooded up to their second floors.

The watery maelstrom uprooted boulders, bent over trees, and jammed structures against the sides of the canyon, crushing them like match sticks. The Colorado and Southern Railroad tracks were twisted like wire. A train with more than one hundred passengers on it was stranded for twenty-four hours when bridges before and behind it were washed away.

But it was the little town of Folsom itself which suffered most terribly from the tidal wave of water and debris. The flood battered and smashed everything in its path. After the calamity, when the stream had subsided, only four business buildings and a few houses remained to mark the site where the once-prosperous town had stood.

With sunrise the next morning, the stunned survivors faced an appalling sight. For miles the stream bed was littered with dead livestock, human victims, and a shambles of jumbled wreckage. The full impact of the tragedy was felt, however, when the grim task of searching for those who had perished began.

As workers began to recover the bodies from the silt, they were shocked to find they had been terribly lacerated by sharp rocks and were completely stripped of their clothing by the force of the current. It was later reported that, for ten miles down the canyon, pieces of torn garments were found thirty feet above the stream bottom, where they were clinging to branches of trees. Identification of the victims was made difficult by their badly mutilated condition. Some women had been scalped when their long hair, traditional in that era, was caught in tree branches as they were swept along.

Bodies were recovered as far as twenty miles downstream. Nine members of two related families perished, including a week-old baby. They were buried in a single grave at Folsom.

But, amazingly the final death toll was only seventeen residents. Sarah Rooke had done her job well, although at the expense of her own life.

One newspaper reporter, perhaps carried away by the drama of the telephone operator's deed, wrote that Sarah's body was found the following Saturday, twelve miles down the canyon, with the headpiece still "fixed on her head and gripping her ear. The telephone cord was broken."[5]

In reality, however, even though searchers combed the tangled debris for miles searching for the town's heroine, Sarah's body could not be found. It was not until six months later, on February 4, 1909, that a rancher, sixteen miles downstream, found her skeleton as he was clearing out a great windrow of drift the flood had left. She was identified by the deformed spine which had made her a cripple.

Sadly, this woman who had sacrificed herself for the people of Folsom was, in a sense, a stranger to them. Although many were familiar with the little lady with the snow white hair and hazel eyes, little was known about her. It was said that she had come to Folsom three years earlier to visit a friend, and had become so enamored with the country that she stayed on.[6] Although she was known as Mrs. Rooke, no husband had accompanied her to Folsom. After her death no living relatives could be found. As a result, the Masons took charge of her burial service.

The news of the selfless telephone operator was reported in newspapers around the nation, but then quickly forgotten. It

(*above*) Memorial plaque on Sarah Rooke's grave cited her heroic devotion to duty and her fellow man. (*below*) Sarah Rooke's grave was heaped with flowers by friends and dignitaries on May 15, 1926, when her monument was unveiled. Some of the mourners were people whose life she had saved. (Author's Collection)

was not until eighteen years later, on May 15, 1926, that a granite monument was erected at her grave in the Folsom cemetery. Throughout the Mountain States region, telephone company employees, four thousand in all, had contributed nickels, dimes, and dollars when they could, to purchase a headstone to honor their fellow worker and her heroic act.

Folsom's flood continued to affect the valley's residents for years. The pain of lost friends and neighbors, and the terror of the night, lived on in survivors's memories. Sometimes more dramatic reminders surfaced. Some years after the disaster, a cowboy riding along the river bed below Folsom saw a brilliant sparkle in the sand. His curiosity piqued, he dismounted and found the bones of a human hand protruding from the sand. On the third finger was a Masonic ring with a diamond setting, like that once worn by the town merchant who had perished.

The flood damaged the town in other ways, too. It was no longer seen as a safe place in which to conduct business. Over the years its population gradually dwindled, until today it has fewer than one hundred residents.

Each year, a few miles to the south, tourists visit the Capulin Mountain National Monument to see one of North America's most symmetrical volcanic cones, from whose heights they can view five states. But the silence in the Folsom graveyard where the selfless Sally Rooke lies is broken only by the soft sighings of the prairie wind blowing through the scant grama grass.

Endnotes:

[1] Clara Toombs Harvey, *Not So Wild the Old West* (Denver: Golden Bell Press, 1961), p. 169.
[2] *Albuquerque Morning Journal*, August 30, 1908.
[3] Harvey, p. 171.
[4] *Albuquerque Morning Journal*, August 30, 1908.
[5] Ibid.
[6] Sally Rooke file, Archives, Telephone Pioneers of America Museum, Albuquerque, New Mexico.

# Selected Bibliography

## Manuscript and Document Sources

Albuquerque Public Library, Special Collections
    U.S. Census records, Hillsboro, N.M. Precinct No. 2, June, 1900.

Highlands University, Las Vegas, New Mexico
    Arrott Collection

Huntington Library, San Marino, California
    Ritch Papers

Martha Liebert Library, Bernalillo, New Mexico
    A. L. Gay letters

Museum of New Mexico Library, Santa Fe, New Mexico
    Unpublished manuscript, "The Law in Their Hands," by Kenneth Fordyce in WPA American Guide File
    Unpublished manuscript, "Stagecoach Days," by Betty Reich, WPA City File
    Unpublished manuscript, "Sadie Orchard, One of New Mexico's Women Stage Drivers," by Clay W. Vaden, New Mexico Writers Project File.

National Archives, Washington, D.C.
    Annual Report of the Secretary of War, 1881
    Military Service Records, Individual Soldiers
    Pension Records, Individual Soldiers
    Record Group 94
        Compiled Service Records of Volunteer Union Soldiers Who Served in Organizations from the Territory of New Mexico.
        Records of the Adjutant General's Office, 1783-1917, Regimental Record Books, 1st Regiment, New Mexico Infantry, Letters Sent and Received and Orders, 1861-66.
    Report No. 104, 43rd Congress, 1st Session, House of Representatives, Washington, D.C.

New Mexico State Records Center and Archives, Santa Fe, New Mexico
    Albert H. Pfeiffer papers.

Telephone Pioneers of America Museum Archives, Albuquerque, New Mexico
    Sally Rooke file

Texas State Library, Austin, Texas
    Photo Archives
    Texas Ranger files

University of New Mexico Library Special Collections, Albuquerque, New Mexico
    Microfilm Collection
        Letters Received by 9th Military District of New Mexico, 1849-1898.

## Newspapers

*Albuquerque Evening Democrat*, New Mexico Territory, 1884.
*Albuquerque Morning Journal*, New Mexico Territory, 1908.
*Albuquerque Journal*, New Mexico Bicentennial Edition, February 1, 1976.
*Albuquerque Tribune*, New Mexico, 1972.
*Albuquerque Weekly News*, New Mexico Territory, 1897.
*Arizona Enterprise*, Florence, 1891.
*El Paso Journal*, Texas, 1978.
*El Paso Times*, Texas, 1938; 1964.
*Grant County Herald*, Silver City, New Mexico Territory, 1877.
*Las Vegas Daily Optic*, New Mexico Territory, 1868; 1881; 1882.
*Mesilla Independent*, New Mexico Territory, 1877.
*Raton Guard*, New Mexico Territory, 1882.
*Raton Comet*, New Mexico Territory, 1882.
*Rio Grande Republican*, Las Cruces, New Mexico Territory, 1885.
*Santa Fe Daily Democrat*, New Mexico Territory, 1882.
*Santa Fe New Mexican*, (daily and weekly) 1863; 1864; 1868; 1869; 1875; 1881.
*Santa Fe Reporter*, New Mexico, 1982.
*Santa Fe Republican*, New Mexico Territory, 1848.
*Santa Fe Weekly Gazette*, New Mexico Territory, 1853; 1858; 1864; 1865; 1869.
*Semi-Weekly Review*, Albuquerque, New Mexico Territory, 1869.
*Silver City Enterprise*, New Mexico Territory, 1886-87.

## Books and Pamphlets

Adams, Rev. Anthony J. *Holy Trinity Church Centennial: 1885-1985*. Trinidad, Colorado: n.p., 1985.

Agnew, S. C. *Garrisons of the Regular Army, New Mexico, 1846-1899*. Santa Fe: Press of the Territorian, 1971.

Beshore, Barron B. *Hippocrates In A Red Vest*. Palo Alto, California: American West Publishing Co., 1973.

Casey, Robert J. *The Texas Border*. New York: The Bobbs-Merrill Co., 1950.

Christiansen, Paige W. *The Story of Mining in New Mexico*. Socorro: New Mexico Bureau of Mines & Mineral Resources, 1974.

Crocchioli, Stanley F. *Desperadoes of New Mexico*. Denver: World Press, 1953.

_____. *The Mora, New Mexico, Story*. Pep, Texas: n.p., 1963.

Fergusson, Erna. *New Mexico: A Pageant of Three Peoples*. New York: Alfred A. Knopf, 1951.

Gustafson, A. M., ed. *John Spring's Arizona*. Tucson: University of Arizona Press, 1966.

Harvey, Clara Toombs. *Not So Wild the Old West*. Denver: Golden Bell Press, 1961.

Horgan, Paul. *Lamy of Santa Fe*. New York: Farrar, Straus and Giroux, 1975.

Howlett, Rev. W. J. *Life of the Right Reverend Joseph P. Machebeuf, D.C.* Pueblo, Colorado: The Franklin Press Co., 1908.

*Illustrated History of New Mexico*. Chicago: Lewis Publishing Company, 1895.

Katz, William Loren. *The Black West*. New York: Doubleday, 1971.

Keleher, William A. *The Fabulous Frontier*. Albuquerque: University of New Mexico Press, 1962.

Kethler, Dorothy. *History of the Harwood Foundation*. Taos, New Mexico, pamphlet.

Leckie, William H. *The Buffalo Soldiers: A Narrative of the Negro Cavalry in the West*. Norman: University of Oklahoma Press, 1967.

Lockwood, Frank C. *The Apache Indians*. Reprint. Lincoln: University of Nebraska Press, 1987.

Marchland, Ernest, ed. *News From Fort Craig, New Mexico, 1863. Civil War Letters of Andrew Ryan, with the First California Volunteers*. Santa Fe, New Mexico: Stagecoach Press, 1966.

*Medal of Honor Recipients, 1863-1973*. Washington: U.S. Government Printing Office, 1973.

Meketa, Charles and Jacqueline. *One Blanket and Ten Days Rations*. Globe, Arizona: Southwest Parks and Monuments Assn., 1980.

Meketa, Jacqueline Dorgan. *Legacy of Honor*. Albuquerque: University of New Mexico Press, 1986.

Meriwether, David. *My Life in the Mountains and On the Plains*. Reprint. Norman: University of Oklahoma Press, 1965.

Mills, W. W. *Forty Years at El Paso*. Chicago: Press of W.B. Conkey Company, 1901.

Nalty, Bernard C. *Strength for the Fight: A History of Black Americans in the Military*. New York: The Free Press, 1986.

Pearce, T. M., ed. *New Mexico Place Names*. Albuquerque: University of New Mexico Press, 1965.

Rakocy, Bill. *Ghosts of Kingston, Hillsboro, New Mexico*. El Paso, Texas: Bravo Press, 1983.

Russell, Marian. *Land of Enchantment, Memoirs of Marian Russell Along the Santa Fe Trail as Dictated to Mrs. Hal Russell*. Reprint. Albuquerque: University of New Mexico Press, 1981.

Sabin, Edwin L. *Kit Carson Days, 1809-1868.* New York: Press of the Pioneers, 1935.

Shalhope, Robert E. *Sterling Price, Portrait of a Southerner.* Columbia: University of Missouri Press, 1971.

Smith, George W. and Charles Judah, eds. *Chronicles of the Gringos.* Albuquerque: University of New Mexico Press, 1968.

Sonnichsen, C. L. *The El Paso Salt War.* El Paso: Texas Western Press, 1973.

_____. *Pass of the North*, Vol. I. El Paso: Texas Western Press, 1968.

Stocking, Hobart E. *The Road to Santa Fe.* New York: Hastings House, 1971.

*The War of the Rebellion, A Compilation of the Official Records of the Union and Confederate Armies.* Series I, Vols. 26 and 34. Washington, D.C.: Government Printing Office, 1880.

Thompson, Jerry. *Henry Hopkins Sibley: Confederate General of the West.* Natchitoches, Louisiana: Northwestern State University Press, 1987.

*Violent New Mexico.* Santa Fe, New Mexico: Ewen Enterprises, n.d.

Wilson, Jane Adeline. *A Thrilling Narrative of the Sufferings of Mrs. Jane Adeline Wilson During Her Captivity Among the Comanche Indians.* Fairfield, Washington: Ye Galleon Press, 1971.

## Articles

Aragon, Ray John, ed. "Mora Intrigue and Murder," *New Mexico Magazine*, 60 (August 1982): 32-34.

Beverley, Mary Frances. "Sadie Orchard Was a Good Ol' Girl." *New Mexico Magazine* (July 1983): 40-42.

Kemper, Troy. "Wall of Water!" *True West Magazine* (January-February 1960): 52.

Lawson, Michael L. "Flora Langermann Spiegelberg: Grand Lady of Santa Fe," *Western States Jewish Historical Quarterly*, 8 (July 1976): 294-95.

Motto, Sytha. "Women's Role In Shaping State Goes Way Back," *Albuquerque Journal* Bicentennial Edition (February 1, 1976): 12.

Potter, Charles D. "Reminiscences of the Socorro Vigilantes," ed. Paige W. Christiansen, *New Mexico Historical Review* 40 No. 1 (January 1965): 29.

Rush, Rita. "'El Chivero' — Merejildo Grijalva," *Arizoniana*, Vol. 1, No. 1 (Spring 1960): 8-10.

Thomlinson, M. H. "The Dragoons and El Paso, 1848," *New Mexico Historical Review* 23 No. 3 (July 1948): 218-21.

Wallace, William S. "Stagecoaching in Territorial New Mexico," *New Mexico Historical Review* 26 No. 2 (April 1957): 92-95.

White, Laura C. Manson. "Albert H. Pfeiffer," *Colorado Magazine*, 10 No. 6 (1935): 217-22.

# Index

Abiquiu, New Mexico 37, 141
Abiquiu Indian Agency 37
Adams, Lieutenant 9
Albuquerque, NM 78, 104, 176
Alvarez, Reyes 87, 90, 98
Anglo prejudices 99
Apache Expedition 34, 58
Apache Pass, AZ 185
Apache Indians 16, 25, 34, 37, 55ff, 153, 184; *rancheria* 59, 189; scouts *photo* 192; tactics 187
Atkinson, John G. 121ff
Avel, Padre Etienne M. 13ff

Bank Exchange Saloon 41, 50
Barela, Chico 129-130
Bargie, Lieutenant L. A. 27
Battle of Valverde 37
Battle of Washita 144
Billy the Kid 67
Black, Robert 67ff
Black Range 148
Black soldiers, prejudice towards 163; on Western frontier 161ff
Blossburg, NM 47
Boggs, Thomas 53, 61
Bosque Redondo Reservation 30, 34
Bowman, Sheriff Mason 139
Bridal Chamber Mine 153
Brothers of Penance 19
Brown and Manzanares Company 174, 180
Buffalo Soldiers 161ff; *sketch* 162
Burbridge, William 42
Burgen, William A. 47, 49-50
Burnett, Lt. George 170-172

California Column 121; Trail 111; Volunteers 34, 185, 188
Camp Nichols, OK 35
Camp Wallen, AZ 188, 190-91
Cañón de Chelly 31, 34, 102; *photos* 32, 103
Capulin Mountain National Monument 202
Carey, Captain Asa 34
Cardis, Luis 127, 130; *photo* 128
Carleton, Maj. Gen. James 9, 12, 31, 34, 35, 58-59, 121, 185; *photo* 10
Carrizal, Mexico 107
Carson, Christopher 'Kit' 28, 35, 53-56, 61; grave *photos* 62
Catholic Church in NM 13ff, 113ff; *photo* 14
Catholic/Jewish relations in Terr. NM 115ff
cavalry, Black 161ff
Cheyenne Indians 35, 164
Chihuahua, Mex. 102, 104, 107-08
Chiricahua Apaches 168
Chiricahua Mountains 185-191
cholera 114
Cimarron, NM 139
Cimarron cut-off 35; Falls 199
Civil War, Black troops 161
Civil War in NM Terr. 53, 79
Clark, Bush 174ff
Clever, Charles 142-43; *photo* 142
Cochise 185, 187, 191
Collins, Col. James L. 12, 76ff
Colorado and Southern RR 199
*Colorado Chiquito* 34
Comanche Indians 1ff, 35, 38, 164
*Comancheros* 164

209

Congressional Medal of Honor, Black recipients   161, 172
Confederate Army of Texans   37, 56, 121
Connolley, Sheriff   175
Coyote, NM   141
Coyotero Indians   60
Creech (Orchard), Sarah Jane 'Sadie'   147ff
Custer, Gen. George A.   144

Dawson, Charles   69ff
de Oñate, Juan   117
Del Norte, CO   39
Doheny, Edward L.   152
Dollman, Deputy Sheriff R. P. 'Pete'   41ff
Doña Ana County, NM   69
Doniphan, Col. Alexander   102
Dry Cimarron River   197

Eaton, Col. E. W.   177; *photo* 177
Eddleston, Hugh   45, 47, 49
Edgar, James C.   85; James M. 76ff; Mrs. James M.   76, 83
El Paso, TX   2, 105, 123ff
El Paso del Norte   3
Ellis, Sheriff Charles   125, 127, 129, 132
Elmoreau, Frenchy   174ff
Fall, Albert Bacon   152
Fessler, Mrs.   90
Fifth Infantry   124
flash floods   196
floods   196
Folsom, NM Terr.   196ff; flood *photo*   198
Fort Bayard, NM   129
Fort Bliss, TX   124
Fort Bowie, AZ   185, 187
Fort Canby, NM   31
Fort Craig, NM   123

Fort Davis, TX   164-65
Fort Garland, CO   35
Fort Goodwin, AZ   58-59
Fort McRae, NM   25-27
Fort Pueblo, CO   55
Fort Selden, NM   123-24
Fort Stanton, NM   72
Fort Stockton, TX   164
Fort Thorn, NM   185
Fort Union, NM   58
Fort Wingate, NM   30, 166
Forty-niner   111
Fountain, Col. Albert J.   71, 75, 156; Henry   156
Frederic Remington   162

Gallegos, Evaristo   141ff
Garrett, Sheriff Pat   157
Georgetown, NM   91-92; *photo* 95
Gay, Albert L.   99ff
Georgetown stage line *photos* 89, 151
Geronimo   58, 153
Gillette, James   177
Good, J. H.   69, 74
Gordon, Tom   176
Grant County, NM   90
Grijalva, Merejildo   184ff; *photo* 192
Grove, Captain   100
Guadalupe Hidalgo Treaty   105
Guadalupe Mountains   2, 165

Hall, Deputy Sheriff Thomas   88ff
Hamilton, P.   71
Hangers, The   176ff
hangings   41ff, 97, 174ff; *photos* 48, 180
Harris, H. W.   42
Harwood Foundation   52, 63
Harwood House *photo*   57

210

Hatch, Col. Edward 165ff;
    *photo* 166
Hayes, Pres. & Mrs. Rutherford
    B. 120
Heath, H. H. 78
Hillsboro, NM 147ff
Hot Springs, NM 158, 160
Howard, Charles 126ff; *photo*
    128
Huachuca Pass, AZ 190

Indian fighting 58, 144, 168
infantry, Black 161ff
influenza 157

Jackson, S. H. 45
jails, territorial 96
Jewish/Catholic relations in
    Terr. NM 115
Jicarilla Apaches 37, 55
journalism, western 135ff
Juarez, Mexico 3

Ka-eet-sah 187
Kaw Indians 117
kidnappings 87; children 184;
    Comanche 1ff
Kingston, NM 147ff
Kiowa Indians 35, 164

*La Conquistadora* 117-19;
    *photo* 118
La Luz, NM 69
Lake Valley, NM 150
Lake Valley, Hillsboro, and
    Kingston Stage Line 152
Lamy, Bishop Jean Baptiste 13,
    17, 113ff; *photos* 16, 118
Lamy Junction 174
Las Cruces, NM 71
*Las Vegas Daily Optic* 138
Latimer, H. J. 45, 49, 51
Lincoln County War 67

Little, Captain E. W. 77, 81, 84
Little Brindle Saloon 44-45, 49
*Los Colgadores* 176
*Los Hermanos de los Penitentes*
    19
Los Lunas, NM 175

Machebeuf, Vicar General
    Joseph 17; *photo* 16
Maes, Refugio 139ff
mail riders, U.S. 188
Mangas Colorado 187
Marile, Silviano 91
Martin, Maritana 141
McAuliff & Ferguson Hall 44
McBride, Frank 130-31
Medal of Honor, Black recipients 161, 172
Mentzer, Gus 41ff
Merriwether, Gov. David 2ff;
    *photo* 10
Mescalero Apaches 2, 164;
    Reservation 168
Mesilla, NM 127
Mexican-American/Anglo relations 91, 99
Mexican-American War 100ff
Mexico City 104
Mills, W. W. 125
Mimbres River, NM 85, 88
mining camps, New Mexico 149
Missouri Volunteers 100, 110
Mister, Fred W. 152, 157
Moqui Indians 30
Mora, NM 13ff
Mortimer, Ranger Sgt. C. E.
    129, 132
Morrison, Major Arthur 27
Moulton, Harvey 47, 49
Mountain Men 53
Mountain States Telephone
    Company employees 202ff
Muache Utes 55

Munnecom, Father Pieter Jan 13ff; *photo* 20

Nana, Chief 170
Narbona, Apache chief 185
Navajos 24, 30ff, 166, 185ff; hogan *photo* 32; scouts at Ft. Wingate 167; *photo* 167
New Mexico Battalion 37
New Mexico Volunteers 25, 28, 31, 34, 37, 185, 188
newspapers, western 135; *photos* 136
Ninth Cavalry 163ff; *photo* Troop "H" at Ft. Wingate 167
Noel 14ff

Ocean Grove Hotel 153
Ojo Caliente, NM 168-69
Ojo Caliente Apaches 152
Old Plume, Apache chief 186
Orchard, James W. 150ff
Orchard, Sarah Jane 'Sadie' Creech 147ff; *photos* 155
Orchard's Mountain Pride 152

Pagosa Springs, CO 25
Palace of the Governors 76ff; floorplan 77; *photo* 79
Payne, Col. Robert 66
Pecos, NM 9
Penitentes 19
Perez, Pilar (see: Saiz) 95ff
Pfeiffer, Albert H. 25; Antonita 37
Pinal Creek 59; Indians 60; Mountains 59
Pinos Altos, NM 88-90
Plains Indians 56, 163
poisonings 14
Polk, Pres. James K. 110
Pope, Gen. John 170

Price, Gen. Sterling 104ff; *photo* 107
priests, French 13, 113
prohibition 158
prostitution, NM Terr. 148
Pueblo Rebellion of 1680 117

*rancheria*, Apache 165, 189, 190; *sketch* 189
Raper, Joseph 71-72; Thomas 66; William 69-72
Raton, NM 41ff; *photo* 46
Rio Grande 25, 123
Rogers, Trumpeter John 171
Rooke, Sarah J. 'Sally' 196ff; *photo* 198; memorial ceremony and monument *photos* 201
Russell, Sheriff Charley 183
Russell, John T. 84
Russell, Lillian 149, 159

St. Vrain, Lt. Col. Ceran 53, 55-56
Saiz, Pilar (see: Perez) 90ff
salt cart *sketch* 126
salt lakes 126
Salt War 127ff
San Carlos Indian Agency 194; Reservation 168
San Elizario, TX 126-29
San Lorenzo, NM 87
Sand Creek Massacre 35
Sandbertson, Delos G. 144
Santa Cruz de Rosales, Chihuahua, battle for 108ff
Santa Fe, NM 7ff, 35, 76ff, 105, 114ff, 174
Santa Fe Cathedral 115; *photo* 118
Santa Fe Rifles 100
Santa Fe Trail 35, 36, 55-56, 99, 111, 113, 117

*Santa Fe New Mexican* 141, 142
*Santa Fe Weekly Gazette* 15, 78, 144
Santa Rita Mountains 88
scalping 4, 144
Sherman, Gen. William T. 120
Sibley, Gen. Henry H. 79
Silver City, NM 64, 88, 90; jail 96; courthouse *photo* 65
*Silver City Enterprise* 65, 91, 135
Simpson, Capt. Smith H. 52ff; *photo* 57; Josefa 61
Sixth Cavalry 169
Smith, William and Jane 2
Socorro, NM 64ff, 94, 104-05, 174ff; *photos* 68, 182
Socorro Committee of Safety 175ff
Socorro Stranglers 174ff
Socorro vigilantes 174ff
Spencer, Deputy Sheriff Peter 91-93, 98
Spiegelberg, Flora 115ff; Lehman 117, 120; Levi 114; Solomon Jacob 114; Willi 117; *photo* of brothers 116
Spiegelberg Stores 114; *photo* 116
Springer, NM 50, 139
stagecoach business 66, 150; drivers, women 152
Steck, Dr. Michael 185
Stockton, Ike 175

Taos, NM 52ff; flagpole 53; *photo* 54
Tays, Lt. John B. 129ff
Teapot Dome Scandal 153
telephone operators, pioneer 196ff
Tenth Cavalry 163
Texas Rangers 128ff, 177
thermal springs 24-25

Tidball, Captain Thomas 186, 188, 195
Tramperos, NM 139
Tres Castillos, Mexico 169
Trias, Gov. Angel, of Chihuahua 108
Trinidad, CO 19ff

Union Army, Black troops 161ff
United States Depository monies 77ff
Ute Campaign (War) of 1855 37, 55
Utes 24, 35, 37; Muache 55

Valdez, Josefa 60-61
Valois, Lt. Gustavus 170-71
Victorio 168-69; *sketch* 170
vigilantes 174ff

wagon trains 2ff
Walker, Major Robert 107, 109, 112
Wallace, NM 67, 74
Walley, Pvt. Augustus 171-72
Warfield, Susan 65
Warm Spring Apaches 168
*Washington Chronicle* 142
Wheater, Sgt. 124
Williams, 1Sgt. Moses 161ff
Wilson, James 2; Jane Adeline 2ff

Yankie Mine 66
Ying, Tom 154ff
Yonkers, 'Bronco Sue' Warfield 64ff

Zubiria, Mexican Bishop 19
Zuñi Pueblo 102; *photo* 103

# FROM MARTYRS TO MURDERERS

The virtues and foibles of the human race are fascinating fodder for any writer. The austere and primitive conditions of life in the Southwest in the last century add extra color to the tales of the saints, sinners, and scalawags of those days.

These were God's unpampered people, living in a harsher time and place. Although these severe conditions were sometimes instrumental in determining specific circumstances, it is only necessary to look beyond the trappings of the story to find the eternal human emotions—heroism, greed, determination, fear, anger, patriotism, revenge, self-indulgence, madness, and all the rest.

In this collection you will find no Billy the Kid, no Sheriff Elfego Baca, no Tunstalls or their Lincoln County War, no Geronimo, and no Pat Garrett. Instead, you will find a fascinating group of lesser-known people who were all caught up in exciting or unusual events.

Each tale has some connection to the New Mexico Territory, although, in some cases, most of the action took place outside its borders in other Southwestern states. The protagonists are as varied as the narratives and their deeds range from the foulest to the finest.

Come, then, and meet "Limpin" John, Sally Rooke, "Bush" Clark and his pal "Frenchy," Padre Etienne Avel, and the rest.

**Jacqueline Dorgan Meketa**, although born in the Panama Canal Zone, has lived in New Mexico for the past forty-one years. A free-lance writer-historian specializing in Territorial New Mexico history, Meketa is the author of *One Blanket and Ten Days Rations*, (with Charles Meketa), *Louis Felsenthal, Citizen-Soldier of Territorial New Mexico*, and *Legacy of Honor—The Life of Rafael Chacón, A Nineteenth-Century New Mexican*, and numerous articles published in national and regional magazines. She and her husband, Charles, reside in Placitas, NM.

Cover design by
John Cole: Cole Graphic Designer, Cerrillos, NM